CLASSIC PEAKS

OF NEW ZEALAND

This book is dedicated to my children, Andrea, Clare, Francis
and Edward. A new generation of mountaineers.

The knife-edge summit of Aoraki/Mt Cook's High Peak, as seen from the Middle Peak. (Photo: Nick Groves/Hedgehog House)

CLASSIC PEAKS

OF NEW ZEALAND

HUGH LOGAN

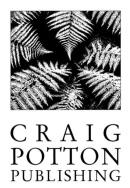

CRAIG
POTTON
PUBLISHING

ACKNOWLEDGEMENTS

I would like to thank the staff of Craig Potton Publishing, in particular Robbie Burton who kept pressure on me to complete tasks, Craig Potton and Tina Delceg, and Dave Chowdhury who did the editing.

Thanks are due to Brian Turner and Barbara Larson at John McIndoe Ltd for their contribution to earlier work published in 1990 which formed the basis of this book.

I want to thank the Canterbury Mountaineering Club for making it possible for me, and thousands of other young people, to get into mountaineering. And I especially want to thank the people I have climbed with over the past thirty years, especially Wilfred Lammerink, Carl Thompson, Lindsay Main, Dave Begg, Bill King and many, many others. We had, and still have, great times, full of humour, grit, triumph, tragedy and good fun.

First published in 2002 by Craig Potton Publishing
Box 555, Nelson, New Zealand
www.craigpotton.co.nz

©2002 Hugh Logan
©credited photographers

Project coordination: Robbie Burton, Tina Delceg, Phillippa Duffy
Editing: David Chowdhury
Filmwork: Image Centre, Auckland, New Zealand
Printed in China through Colorcraft Ltd., Hong Kong

ISBN 0 908802 88 9

CONTENTS

Nearing the summit of Mt Silberhorn, en route to Mt Tasman, with the Grand Plateau below. (Photo: Gottlieb Braun-Elwert)

PREFACE

Mountains have always been part of my life. At the age of five, I began skiing in the Canterbury ranges, and soon after spent summers trout fishing with my father in the lakes of those ranges. As a teenager, I became consumed by a desire to explore and climb the Torlesse mountains and Arthurs Pass peaks. From there, trips to the great ranges of the Southern Alps led on to a life of climbing. This experience revealed to me the enormous richness of New Zealand's mountain heritage. Mountains are a part of what makes up the character of a people. Mountains are visible, and often dominant, in every city and every town in the country. For New Zealanders, their sense of place is anchored by their mountain connections.

A personal enthusiasm for mountains has driven me to record the stories of the great peaks of New Zealand. I have selected seventeen mountains as the classic peaks: mountains which because of their size, their dominance and their challenge have attracted people to them.

Central to the stories of New Zealand's classic peaks has been the history of mountaineering. It developed in the late nineteenth century when young people seeking adventure and explorations developed a distinctive indigenous style of climbing. New Zealand's mountains are characterised by a harsh, fast-changing climate and remoteness. Wind is ever-present – the gale-force northwesterly in particular. Climbers have to be self-reliant, hazard conscious, and able to carry both food and shelter for at least several days. Despite these pre-conditions, local mountaineers have become accomplished world class climbers. In 1895 the ascent of the North Ridge of Aoraki/Mt Cook rivalled the climbs in Europe of the time, while the recent winter ice-face routes in the Southern Alps are internationally cutting edge.

What motivates climbers? It is the physical and mental challenge rather than the concept of conquest. It is also a sense of satisfaction in completing a route, of reaching the summit as the culmination of a journey. Underlying all this is the beauty and power of the surrounding landscape. New Zealand mountains contain an amazing diversity of forest, alpine meadows, scree, rock and glaciers. Three-thousand-metre peaks rise abruptly out of eastern grasslands or western rainforests, and from most summits the ocean is no more than twenty kilometres away. Climbing in New Zealand is a soulful and complete experience.

AORAKI/MT COOK

...Mt Cook towering over all, blocking up the vista to the right with his pyramid of rock and ice, and forming one of the grandest scenes of the southern hemisphere. Rev. W S Green, The High Alps of New Zealand

One mountain surpasses all others in New Zealand. It is Aoraki. From its summit you have the awesome feeling that you are on the pinnacle of everything, the other great peaks around you, the plains to the east and the forest to the west, and beyond them the oceans; there is nothing between you and the sky.

It is difficult to encompass in a short space the enormously rich story that surrounds this mountain. It is steeped in mythology; it has been the scene of struggle, triumph, joy, high comedy and tragedy.

Aoraki/Mt Cook is the highest peak in the Southern Alps – an area of continuous mountain building at the margins of the Pacific and the Indo-Australian crustal plates. Oceanic sediments laid down millions of years ago have been compressed, folded and thrust up to form the major part of the Southern Alps. Moisture from the surrounding oceans driven primarily by fierce westerly winds has almost matched the uplift with a continuous process of erosion, intensified over the past 100,000 years by a series of ice ages forming great valley glaciers and ice-caps. The present 18 kilometre long Tasman Glacier and shorter Hooker Glacier surrounding Aoraki/Mt Cook are tiny remnants of great rivers of ice that stretched far out to the East Coast. These geological processes have given us a mountain flanked to the west by the narrow and spectacular Hooker Glacier and on the east by the Grand Plateau and Ball Glaciers, both feeders to the lower part of the Tasman Glacier. And the mountain building, or mountain falling, is ongoing. Major rock falls were noted on the south side of the mountain in the 1880s. On 14 December 1991, at about midnight, the mountain let go more than six million cubic metres of rock down 2,700 metres of its east face, the avalanche then travelling six kilometres across the Tasman Valley. The summit was lowered by 12 metres.

Just as modern science has given us an explanation of the origins of the mountain, so too has Maori legend woven a layer of mythology. At the deepest level Aoraki, the cloud in the sky (a name existing in different forms amongst the most notable of peaks throughout Polynesia), was the son of Rangi, the Sky Father. At another level Aoraki was a celestial explorer who with his three brothers Rakiroa, Rakirua and Rarakiroa were wrecked in their canoe. As the canoe listed they climbed onto its side and were turned to stone. The canoe, or waka, represented the South Island, and the four explorers became the highest peaks of the central Southern Alps.

The prominent role of Aoraki in Maori legend is obvious. The mountain is visible for much of the length of the West Coast, and the East Coast Maori ventured regularly into the Waitaki basin

Left: Aoraki/Mt Cook from the north, with the Zurbriggen Ridge on the left and the standard Linda Glacier route in the centre. (Photo: Craig Potton)
Above: Climbing through the summit rocks, Aoraki/Mt Cook. (Photo: Nick Groves)

Marmaduke Dixon (left) and Tom Fyfe, on reaper blade skis, Grand Plateau, 1894. (Photo: G Mannering, W A Kennedy Collection, Canterbury Museum)

from at least 1000 AD on, first to hunt the moa – and in the process burned the mixed totara/cedar forest that grew in the region – and later every summer to catch and preserve smaller birds for winter food in their coastal settlements. Aoraki was a constant companion, gleaming under a wide summer sky.

Europeans followed. Captain Stokes named the 'stupendous mountain' after James Cook during Stokes's coast survey of New Zealand in 1851. Pastoralists followed the route of alleged sheep rustler James MacKenzie and by the late 1850s hardy sheep farmers, like Nicolo Radove and Andrew Burnett, settled in the Tasman

Valley to live year round through hot summers and iron-hard winters within sight of the great peak. And soon after the pastoralists came the surveyors like Julius von Haast to map the geology and vegetation, and Edward Sealy to carry out triangulations. To all of them Aoraki/Mt Cook was a centre of attraction.

In the words of pastoralist Samuel Butler:

If a person says he thinks he has seen Mount Cook, you may be quite sure that he has not seen it. The moment it comes into sight the exclamation is 'That is Mount Cook!' – not 'That must be Mount Cook!'

Butler prophesised that:

There is a glorious field for the members of the Alpine Club here. Mount Cook awaits them, and he who first scales it will be crowned with undying laurels...

For his part, Butler doubted anyone would climb it!

Butler, of course, was wrong. The first attempt on Aoraki/Mt Cook was launched from 15,000 kilometres away in Europe by the Rev. William Green, Swiss hotelier Emil Boss, and guide Ulrich Kaufmann. It was an epic adventure. They sailed to New Zealand and then early in 1882 travelled by train and horse and cart to Birch Hill sheep station. From there the trio had to struggle through untracked scrub beside the Tasman Glacier. Despite a number of false starts they finally struck up the Linda Glacier high onto the mountain. Then with light fading, a freshening storm and the summit a mere 50 metres or less away, they turned for home satisfied in their minds at least that they had climbed the peak. To those who followed however, the issue was still in doubt.

Green's attempt on Aoraki/Mt Cook inspired a young New Zealander from Christchurch, George Mannering. Mannering and the band of climbers he drew around him formed the nucleus of New Zealand's first mountaineers. Their primary objective was to complete the ascent of Aoraki/Mt Cook, but in the process they founded the sport of mountaineering in this country. In 1887 Mannering, Marmaduke Dixon and C H Inglis climbed up the Haast Ridge beside the Hochstetter Icefall and established the fa-

Aoraki/Mt Cook at sunset from the Hermitage. (Photo: Craig Potton)

mous bivouac site (below Green's campsite, and where the Haast Hut now stands). In 1891 Mannering and Dixon repeated Green's ascent almost exactly and like Green they were forced back just short of the summit with darkness coming on. By the mid 1890s reaching the summit had become an obsession with Mannering and his companions.

At lower altitudes things were becoming easier for the climbers. In 1884 a cob accommodation house had been built by Frank Huddleston at the junction of the Mueller and Hooker valleys. This building, named the Hermitage, was the forerunner of three hotels, one where the cob cottage stood, and the others, the present Hermitage and its predecessor, two kilometres down valley. With the arrival of tourists came other facilities – a wire cage and later bridges over the Hooker River. In 1891 a track was cut through the previously jungle-like matagouri of the Tasman Valley and most important of all, a two-room hut, Ball Hut, was built on the moraine wall at the junction of the Ball and Tasman glaciers.

With these facilities, attempts to climb Aoraki/Mt Cook were redoubled. News that an Englishman, Edward Fitzgerald and Swiss guide, Mattias Zurbriggen, would arrive to attempt the peak in early 1895 aroused a frenzy of activity amongst local climbers. At least five separate attempts on Aoraki/Mt Cook via the Linda Glacier failed (Dixon even fashioned sets of skis from reaper blades to cope with the soft snow). Finally, in December 1894 two of Mannering and Dixon's protégés, Tom Fyfe and George Graham, abandoned the Linda route and explored the western approaches to the mountain. On 20 December the pair climbed from a camp on a rock spur at the foot of the West Ridge leading to the Low Peak. They skirted just under the Low Peak summit at 1 p.m. and reached the Middle Peak. But before them lay a kilometre of knife-like corniced ridge. Reluctantly they turned and by that evening were back in the Hermitage. Undaunted however, they immediately returned to the attack with 19-year-old Jack Clarke. This time they camped on the glacier at the head of the Hooker Valley.

Then, on Christmas Day 1894 they tackled a steep, rock-swept couloir leading up to a narrow col connecting Mt Dampier to Aoraki/Mt Cook's North Ridge. Above the col the ridge rose in three rock steps, the last one in particular requiring a good standard of rock-climbing. Thus it was that three self-taught New Zealand climbers, joined by a hemp rope, and shod in leather clinker-lined boots, reached the summit at 1 p.m., having completed an ascent which even today is regarded as a major achievement.

The first ascent of Aoraki/Mt Cook marked the maturing of the sport of mountaineering in New Zealand. In the years that followed there have been over 1,000 ascents by more than 40 different routes. To describe every route would be a wearisome task. There are however, certain climbs that stand as landmarks in the history of the mountain and reflect the development of the sport and New Zealand society. These climbs are the traverse of the three summits of Aoraki/Mt Cook, the East Ridge, the East Face and the Caroline Face.

The traverse, known as the Grand Traverse, was the culminating feat of an era known as the golden age of New Zealand climbing. Between 1894 and 1914 all the major summits in the area were climbed. In the glorious summer of 1894–95, Aoraki/Mt

Harold Porter on the Grand Traverse, 1927. (Photo: Marcel Kurz, W A Kennedy Collection, Canterbury Museum)

Cook, Tasman, Sefton, Haidinger and Silberhorn were all climbed, while Mattias Zurbriggen, accompanied by the Hermitage manager, John Adamson, climbed the North East Ridge of Aoraki/Mt Cook to make the second ascent. A lull in activity followed until the early 1900s when tourism began to expand, the Hermitage grew as a popular resort, and the profession of guiding flourished under the leadership of chief guides, Jack Clarke and Peter Graham. Graham, in particular, established a high standard of professional-

ism and expertise and built around him a team of guides capable of tackling the hardest routes. Fyfe, for example, linked himself irrevocably with Aoraki/Mt Cook through the first ascent (he climbed the mountain three times, traversing Zurbriggens Ridge in 1906, and climbing the western Earles Ridge in 1911). Graham himself climbed over forty new routes in the district including five new routes on Aoraki/Mt Cook. He was aided by buoyant economic times and a small but steady stream of wealthy clients. People such as Lawrence Earle, Bernard Head and Samuel Turner were able to employ Graham for the whole summer and only climb when conditions were perfect. They needed to be, for climbers then had few means of safe belaying and relied on the skill and strength of the guides to hew enormous lines of steps up the snow and ice. Crampons were not worn.

Amongst those who came to climb was a young Australian woman, Freda du Faur. Over three summers she developed into an excellent climber and in the process overcame enormous obstacles against women attempting such feats. In 1910 Peter and Alec Graham guided her up Earles Ridge in just six hours, and she became the first woman to climb Aoraki/Mt Cook. Based on this experience the Grahams determined to attempt the big prize of that time, the Grand Traverse.

The attempt took place in January 1913. Alec Graham was not available and his place was taken by fellow West Coaster and guide, Darby Thomson, a short man of tireless energy and irrepressible humour. The attempt was made on 3 January from a bivouac near the foot of the west ridge of the Low Peak. They made a fast ascent to the Low Peak and at 7 a.m. set out along the two kilometre ridge over the Middle Peak to the High Peak. The first section, to Porter's Col (named later after an English climber, Harold Porter) was straightforward and in any event they were following the path used by Fyfe and Graham on their ascent of the Middle Peak 16 years before. But in this instance, there was a fierce schrund up which Graham had to cut foot and handholds. From the Middle Peak lay their true challenge. A sinuous, corniced and spectacu-

Looking along the final rope length of the Grand Traverse to the pinnacle summit of the High Peak of Aoraki/Mt Cook. (Photo: Ned Norton)

Moonrise above the North Ridge and Sheila Face, Aoraki/Mt Cook.
(Photo: Craig Potton)

larly beautiful ridge wound away to the High Peak, plunging 1,800 metres on the right down the east face and curling off left in a huge sweep to the Hooker Glacier. Freda du Faur recalled:

More than once as we ascended an icy shiver ran down my spine as the ice axe sank deeply into the overhanging cornice and on withdrawal, disclosed through the tiny hole the awful gap between us and the glacier thousands of feet below.

It was ice all the way and Graham cut steps for five hours solidly, relieved by Darby Thomson for 20 minutes. The final knife-edge sweep of ice to the summit required special care, but at 1.30 p.m. they stepped onto the summit, the 'glorious aerial ice-ridge' behind them.

The traverse of Aoraki/Mt Cook caused a considerable sensation. The presence of Freda du Faur in the party made newspaper headlines, astounded that a woman should accomplish such an arduous feat. Less prominent in the publicity, but more enduring, was the fact that Graham, Thomson and du Faur had pioneered a route that will always thrill any mountaineer. Sadly, just over a year later Darby Thomson was killed descending the Linda Glacier. Thomson had made his name on numerous top quality climbs,

including the second ascent of the Linda Glacier route guiding Samuel Turner and accompanied by second-guide and member of Poutini Ngai Tahu, George Bannister. Thomson, a skilled and enthusiastic West Coaster was descending Aoraki/Mt Cook with guide Jock Richmond and client Sydney King, having made his fifth ascent of the mountain. They were overwhelmed by an avalanche – Mt Cook's first victims.

Twenty-five years elapsed between the Grand Traverse and the next new route on Aoraki/Mt Cook – the 1800 metre East Ridge – which bisects the huge eastern flanks of the mountain, rising from the Grand Plateau to the Middle Peak. The East Ridge presented a challenge to the climbers of the 1930s. Those to climb it were two of the finest climbers of their time, Dan Bryant and Lud Mahan. Bryant was a schoolteacher, with a string of first ascents to his credit, and a member of the 1935 Everest expedition (his strong performance led directly to the invitation to New Zealanders to participate in the post-war British Everest expeditions). Mahan, also a teacher, spent his summers guiding at the Hermitage. The pair attempted the route in 1933 but were turned back halfway by soft snow. In January 1938 they returned again. This time they bivouacked on the climb, about 100 metres up the ridge in a little eyrie overlooking the vast Caroline Face. The alternative would have meant starting up from the Haast Ridge Hut, over three kilometres away and 700 metres lower. As a result Bryant and Mahan got away at 3.40 a.m. just as dawn was breaking. Unlike their attempt five years earlier, conditions on the lower part of the ridge were excellent. Firm snow allowed them to crampon their way to a small peaklet on the ridge at 3,050 metres. Dan Bryant wrote:

It was here that we struck an exceedingly sharp undulating ridge, leading from this point into the wall of the mountain. Falling away almost sheer on either side, and offering little or no anchorage should the crest give way.

And ominously, conditions on the mountain gave way from firm to unstable snow, some nearly thigh deep, interspersed with sections of hard blue ice. The last 500 metres of the East Ridge are

The gigantic 2,000 metre-high Caroline Face, with the standard ascent route straight up the middle rib. (Photo: Craig Potton)

Climbers return back across the Grand Plateau, with the East Face behind.
(Photo: Colin Monteath/Hedgehog House)

a near continuous ice slope hanging at the top of a 2,500-metre drop down the Caroline Face. It took Bryant and Mahan six hours of careful climbing, using ice pick belays and wrought steel point crampons, linked by a hemp rope. However, at five past three in the afternoon they cut through a cornice onto the Middle Peak:

...the strain was off and yet another virgin arête was mastered. It was a moment of intense satisfaction as we realised that yet another page in our book of mountaineering memories had been filled. It is such moments as these that make the sport what it is.

Other ridges were climbed after the East Ridge: the South Ridge by Harry Ayres, Mick Sullivan, Ruth Adams and Ed Hillary in 1947, and the Bowie Ridge by Hamish MacInnes, Peter Robinson and Dick Irwin in 1956. Both may be more difficult than the ear-

lier routes but they lack the classical lines and the big mountain exposure. The East Ridge remains the best ridge climb on Aoraki/Mt Cook.

Besides the ridge, Aoraki/Mt Cook possesses five major faces. The northern Sheila Face and the western Hooker Face are just under 1,000 metres high. The Hooker Face is the easiest, first climbed in 1956. The Sheila Face is entirely rock and leads directly to the High Peak. Although it was not climbed until 1967, and is rather difficult in sections, it is friendly and sunny. The South Face looks directly onto the Hermitage. It is all ice runnels and hanging ice cliffs. Paradoxically, it now has 12 different routes up it, with some of the hardest ice-climbing on the mountain. The South Face, and particularly the routes on its right side, are a *tour de force* involving real difficulties, and some danger!

The two remaining faces on Aoraki/Mt Cook are the biggest. The East Face is 1,800 metres high, the southeast or Caroline Face is 2,500 metres. Neither is as steep or as difficult as the South and Sheila faces. Ascents of both, however, have marked epochs in New Zealand mountaineering development, and thus deserve attention amongst the great routes on the mountain.

In the 1950s the East Face was regarded as the foremost mountaineering challenge in New Zealand. It was a long climb and prone to bad rockfall. Understandably, climbers held concerns for the safety of the climb, particularly as ice techniques and protection were not good at that time.

Many climbers secretly harboured thoughts of climbing it. In 1956 Hamish MacInnes soloed Zurbriggens Ridge and cached food on the summit in preparation for an attempt that never eventuated. Early in 1960 Mike Gill, Ian Cave and John Nicholls eyed up the face. Gill wrote:

None of us were enthusiastic. There was ice everywhere and a coating of fresh snow, there was rockfall, gaping slots at the foot of the face.

And so came November 1961. A party comprising Peter Farrell, Don Cowie and Vic Walsh rushed down to the Hermitage from Christchurch with the promise of good weather. Here they teamed up with Lyn Crawford who worked locally as a guide and had judged that conditions for the climb were perfect – a good snow covering, no ice, and cool temperatures to keep the rockfall at bay. The party flew by ski-plane to the Grand Plateau and set up a tent camp near where the Grand Plateau hut was to be built two years later. At 10 p.m. on 20 November Farrell, Cowie, Crawford and Walsh left their camp and cramponned across the plateau to the East Face under bright moonlight. The first third of the face was climbed quickly. The four climbers were amongst the best in the country; Cowie had developed cramponning to a fine art, Farrell had limitless reserves of drive and determination, while Crawford and Walsh provided the enthusiasm. They needed these qualities. The upper

parts of the face were sheathed in hard ice. They were forced to alternate between climbing on the front points of their crampons and cutting steps. Ice pitons anchoring each belay took a multitude of hammer blows to place. Moreover, morning sun loosened rocks.

The last 200 metres were the steepest of all. Below them stretched the face they had just climbed. Rope length by rope length they scratched their way up the iron-hard ice to a shallow cornice. 'At long last we were at the top of Cook's magnificent east face. Straddling the ridge I gazed down on the Grand Plateau, a very gratifying moment', wrote Farrell.

The climb of the East Face was a gigantic breakthrough. It was a route that had tantalised mountaineers and now the problem had been overcome.

South of the East Face lies Aoraki/Mt Cook's greatest feature, the enormous Caroline Face. The Caroline is not as steep as the East Face, or a number of other faces of Mt Cook. But 2,500 metres high and guarded by ice cliffs, it scowled at earlier climbers, warning them away. As far back as the 1930s it was recognised that an obvious route lay up a series of arêtes running up the centre of the face. But it was also recognised that the lower half of the climb would entail running a gauntlet of unstable ice cliffs, while there was also another daunting ice cliff which cut across the face at halfway. On top of all this, the climb would undoubtedly entail at least one bivouac, and such activities were looked upon justifiably as dangerous.

In the 1950s new equipment and new attitudes increased interest in the Caroline Face. But still no one drew near. Only in November 1962, a year after the East Face climb, did Don Cowie and Peter Farrell try the climb. After one aborted attempt, they reached the large ice cliff at half height. To their dismay it was over 50 metres high and overhanging. They resorted to artificial climbing, leap-frogging their small collection of ice pitons. But after three hours, and only reaching halfway, they turned back. The following year, 1963, Michael Goldsmith and John Cousins set out for the climb leaving a note in Ball Hut that they would 'have a look at the Caroline Face'. They disappeared in a huge storm that swept the mountain for ten days. A month later Farrell and Cowie returned, accompanied this time by Lyn Crawford and Brian Hearfield. Again they reached the large cliff and fixed a rope to two-thirds height before bivouacking. In the morning however, the mountain struck back. An ice avalanche roared over the bivouac and felled Crawford. The other three spent the day shepherding him safely off the mountain. Then, for four years, the Caroline Face was left alone.

In the late 1960s a new generation of climbers began to arrive at the Hermitage. Young, impecunious, they were prepared to spend their summers living on nothing but climbing. The Caroline Face was a perfect match for their brash, aggressive approach. In 1968 Peter Farrell teamed up with Pete Gough but only managed a short part of the lower section before a storm moved in. The following month Gough tried again, with George Harris. Again, they made little impression on the face. The following year they had another go with Dave White and John Glasgow. This time they reached the ice cliff, but not before an horrendous battle with a huge crevasse lower on the face. Nevertheless, a vicious nor'west storm drove them from the face, at times the wind blasting the climbers over on the glacier below.

With such a burst of activity, it seemed only a matter of time before the Caroline succumbed, particularly as more and more climbers were becoming interested.

So, with competition running hot, a foursome of Gough, Harris, Glasgow and Wellington climber Graeme Dingle agreed that in 1970–71 they would make an all-out assault on the face. A large anticyclone moved onto the country in early November, and Gough and Glasgow, living in Christchurch, drove to Mount Cook to investigate conditions. They were perfect. The following sequence of events is rather confused and controversial. Gough and Glasgow decided not to wait for Harris and Dingle. Instead they went straight onto the face. The first the Wellingtonians knew of it was on a national radio news report, followed by television coverage. Climb-

ing on Mt Cook had reached the electronic age, and the Caroline provided a superb spectacle. Dingle and Harris were furious. They took off immediately for Mt Cook. By this time Gough and Glasgow were halfway up.

The ice cliff, which had so bothered earlier parties, was in better condition and Gough led it with ease. Above them lay the untouched upper half of the face. It was not steep, but it stretched interminably upwards. Gough and Glasgow ground their way up until they struck the top icefield. Grey ice barred the way, but to their left fingers of snow streaked up the ice. The pair tensioned across the ice and gingerly tiptoed up the snow. Extreme tiredness was taking its toll. But at 6 p.m. they reached the summit ridge between the Low and Middle Peaks. Gough recorded:

We just soaked up the setting sun. 'You know we've really done it'. It was hard to believe, but we had. Emotion ran pretty high – 'Glasgow, you're a bit of a prick but sometimes I almost love you'.

Gough and Glasgow descended the next day to the Hermitage and massive media adulation. For their part, it was entirely unexpected, but it kept them fed for a week. In the meantime, Dingle and Harris were wearily following in their footsteps up the face.

In 1999 there was a fascinating sequel to the Caroline Face story when human remains and part of a climber's crash helmet were found in the lower Hooker Glacier. Inside the helmet was the name Cousins! How had the bodies of two climbers who had set out to attempt the Caroline Face 36 years earlier ended up on the other side of the mountain? The state of the equipment led some to believe they had died in a bivouac. Had they climbed the face and then died in the horrendous storm that lashed the mountain the day after they set out? Quite possibly. The movement of the bodies meant they must have died high on the Hooker side of the mountain. And to get there they would have either climbed the Caroline Face, or the East Ridge (Peter Farrell was reported to have seen them low on the Face on the day they left Ball Hut).

The ascent of the Caroline was a major landmark in climbing

Sunrise on the level arête midway up the East Ridge of Aoraki/Mt Cook. (Photo: Mike Freeman/Hedgehog House)

on Aoraki/Mt Cook and in New Zealand. It was not an exceptionally difficult climb, although it did require great stamina. It has since had more ascents than the East Face, has been climbed in winter, and was soloed by Bill Denz in 1973. Denz's climb, via a new route, and in a storm, was accomplished in the remarkable time of nine hours. One day someone will ski down it. But the ascent broke a psychological barrier. Over the next three years most of the great unclimbed faces in the Aoraki/Mt Cook district were climbed. Just as the first ascent of the mountain in 1894 marked a beginning for mountaineering in general in New Zealand, so too did the first ascent of the Caroline Face mark the beginning of the modern face climbing era.

All of the major features on Aoraki/Mt Cook have now been climbed. New adventure is found in attempting the striking features of each face though. Bill McLeod demonstrated his dominance of the New Zealand alpine climbing scene in the late 1980s and early 1990s by soloing in winter most of Aoraki/Mt Cook's major classic routes. Beginning in 1984, over the next seven years McLeod soloed in winter Earles Ridge, the East Ridge, the Sheila Face's Central Buttress, the Caroline Face, and the South Ridge. With Hugh Widdowson he climbed the Hooker Face (in summer) and in the winter of 1989 he climbed two other routes on the Sheila Face. In July 1991, McLeod capped off this amazing record by climbing the Bowie Ridge, a new line up a buttress on the left of the East Face (Rumblestiltzkin, with Peter Dickson), as well as a direct ascent of the North Ridge.

In a remarkable day in December 1986 Rob Hall flew his parapente from the summit, landing at Ball Hut seven minutes later. The same time as Hall was flying, Mark Whetu was skiing down Zurbriggens Ridge: not the first ski descent of Mt Cook – that had been done in 1982 by Geoff Wayatt and John Blenner-hassett – but certainly the most daring. Whetu departed the summit just before Hall flew off. He skied down the ice-cap and the steep 50° gully that Green's party had struggled up over a century earlier, and traversed over to Zurbriggens Ridge. Then, taking a deep breath, he launched off down the 1000 metres of snow face – an epoch marking event in New Zealand ski-mountain descents.

Coincidentally, both Hall and Whetu were to make their names on Mt Everest. Hall, who climbed and guided the world's highest peak five times, died in tragic circumstances just above the South Summit trying to bring a sick client down in a storm. Whetu climbed the North Ridge of Everest twice. On the second time, he bivouacked on the summit. On the second day, during the descent his companion died slowly from cerebral oedema, Whetu endured a second night out, but survived.

The new adventures of winter, parapenting and skiing show the mountain's continuing strong attraction. The slowly rising death toll (now over 30) marks the unwary, the unready and the unlucky. For Aoraki/Mt Cook is no easy summit. Even by its simplest route, the climber must have some understanding and ability in mountaineering and be prepared for a long outing. But to stand on the summit of New Zealand is an experience none will forget. Tom Fyfe's closing sentence in his description of the first ascent captures the feelings of all Aoraki/Mt Cook climbers:

As we lay, idly watching the northwest clouds swirling overhead, our trials were all forgotten, and I regretfully thought – there is but one Aorangi.

HIGH PEAK   MIDDLE PEAK   PORTER LOW
COL PEAK

SHEILA FACE

UPPER EMPRESS
SHELF

LOWER EMPRESS
SHELF

Photo: Peter Morath

AORAKI/MT COOK
Classic Route: West Ridge and Grand Traverse

Access: From the Mount Cook Village ascend the Hooker Glacier to either Gardiner Hut (this takes 5 hours) or Empress Hut (this takes 8 hours). At 2,500 metres, Empress Hut permits a faster start to the climb.

The Climb: From the Lower Empress Shelf, ascend a prominent couloir (the North West Couloir) or the northwest buttress. The couloir broadens out higher up and leads onto the upper West Ridge at 3,200 metres. Alternatively, it is easy to climb the rocks left of the upper part of the couloir. The upper West Ridge is usually straightforward snow slopes to the Low Peak at 3,595 metres.

From the Low Peak, begin the Grand Traverse which links the Low Peak, Mid-dle Peak and High Peak. The two-kilometre-long ridge is initially over rocks near the Low Peak, then along a broad ridge to Porter's col and up a snow slope to the Middle Peak (3,742 metres). Beyond the Middle Peak the ridge narrows and is heavily cor-niced to the east, especially on the final steep section to the High Peak (3,754 metres).

Descend from the High Peak down the North East ridge, summit rocks (one rappel) and the crevassed and avalanche-threatened Linda Glacier.

First Ascent: Peter Graham, Freda du Faur, Darby Thomson: January 1913.

Grade 3

Two climbers on the last 300 metres of Mt Tasman's Silberhorn Ridge. (Photo: Nick Groves/Hedgehog House)

MT TASMAN

At 3,498 metres Mt Tasman is at once both the physical culmination and the crowning glory of the Main Divide of the Southern Alps. Mt Tasman is the queen of New Zealand's mountains, a beautiful white spire complementing the bulky mass of the higher nearby Aoraki/Mt Cook. Any approach to Tasman should be made carefully and with due deference. For Tasman is the premier ice climb in the country.

If I were to wish that one New Zealand mountain were to stand alone and all others disappear, it would be Mt Tasman ... it is the mountaineer's mountain, yielding experiences which are no doubt etched onto the memories of all who have ventured onto it. Bill Denz

From the east, Mt Tasman has been described as 'a soaring white canvas, forever flying across an infinite blue ocean', so few are the outcrops visible on its east face and ridges. To the west is a complex array of faces and ridges, in particular the remote Balfour Glacier and the steep ramparts of Tasman's Hidden and Balfour faces. Finally, there is the southern ridge, a knife edge arête of 250 metres 'a vision to make the heart of a mountaineer thrill with the anticipation of battle'.

Tasman was named by explorer and geologist, Julius von Haast after the first European to visit New Zealand. Indeed, Tasman's first sight of land could well have been the mountain named after him. His journal of 13 December 1642 stated: 'Towards noon saw a large land, uplifted high'. Tasman's two small ships, the *Heemskerck* and the *Zeehaen* were about 90 kilometres off the West Coast. Tasman's predecessors had other names for the mountain though. In the Aoraki legend, Tasman is Rarakiroa (Long Unbroken Line). Rarakiroa was a brother of Aoraki and one of the explorers who became stone when their canoe was wrecked. European settlers on the West Coast, somewhat prosaically, were content to describe the mountain simply as 'the Dome'.

As the second highest mountain in New Zealand Mt Tasman would have obvious mountaineering interest, even if it wasn't such a spectacular peak. Thus, when Aoraki/Mt Cook was climbed in 1894, attention obviously turned on Tasman. Edward Fitzgerald, a young English gentleman, with guide Mattias Zurbriggen of Macugnaga, Italy, determined to climb it after being thwarted on Cook by New Zealanders making the first ascent. In mid January 1895 they set up camp on the Haast Ridge leading up from the Tasman Glacier to the expanse of the Grand Plateau, choosing the historic bivouac site used by Mannering and his companions when they had made their attempts on Aoraki/Mt Cook in the early 1890s. The next day, Fitzgerald, Zurbriggen and local climbers Jack Clarke and A M Ollivier tackled the southern arête on the East Face. Storm drove them back. On 5 February Fitzgerald, Zurbriggen and Clarke returned to the attack. In the early light of morning they crossed the Grand Plateau to the foot of the ridge they had attempted earlier and which led up to a peak, later called Mt Silberhorn, on the

Starting up the North Shoulder section of the North Ridge of Mt Tasman after traversing Mt Lendenfeld and Engineer Col below. (Photo: Nick Groves)

Jack Cox (left) and Joe Fleurty on the summit after the first ascent of the North Ridge, 1932. (Photo: Jack Pope, A C Graham collection)

south arête of Tasman. Zurbriggen and Fitzgerald had crampons, and Zurbriggen fixed inch-long spikes into Clarke's shoes. Their second breakfast consisted of a box of sardines and a few fruit biscuits but Clarke, showing his distinct cultural heritage, demolished a quantity of mutton and a pot of jam. Fiery and energetic, Zurbriggen hacked steps up and above the Silberhorn, cutting briefly out onto the East Face to bypass a steep ice wall. They stepped onto the summit at 1 p.m. with a nor'westerly storm breaking. The summit, a sharp icy knob with only just room for the three of them to stand, was no place to linger. They hurried back down the staircase of steps Zurbriggen had hacked in the ice, taking a total of 16 hours for the whole climb. Fitzgerald did not rate their Tasman climb in the same category as his ascent of nearby Mt Sefton, but whereas Sefton has an easy approach from the west, the Silberhorn route to Mt Tasman was subsequently to prove the least difficult way to the summit. Another point Fitzgerald made was to doubt whether the mountain would ever be climbed without crampons. In this he was wrong.

The people to prove Fitzgerald wrong were the Graham brothers, Peter and Alec. Tasman held a special place in the hearts of these two West Coasters. Their climbing instincts had been kindled on the many evenings of their youth spent at their home on Three Mile Beach gazing at the flames of sunset slowly dying on the summit of Tasman. In March 1912, they set out to guide that pioneer of female mountaineers, Freda du Faur, up Tasman. Du Faur was an excellent climber, and in the Graham brothers she had the best guides in the country. Indeed, du Faur's opinion of the Grahams, and Peter in particular, approached adulation. None of the party wore crampons but the Grahams were step-cutters extraordinaire, brought up in the West Coast bushmen's traditions, who with long handled and enormously heavy adzed ice axes could undertake hours of cutting huge bucket steps in ice. The Tasman climb in particular was a step-cutting marathon and the final arête to the summit, described by du Faur as 'a knife-edge of 1,000 feet at the most appalling angle I have ever beheld or imagined', took Alec Graham hours of work, a step-cutting effort to awe today's climber. Alec is reputed to have muttered as he cut onto the summit 'Tasman, I've got you', so much was his determination satisfied.

The difficult nature of Mt Tasman is testified to most eloquently by comparing the record of ascents with those of Aoraki/ Mt Cook. For 20 years after their first ascents Tasman was climbed seven times, Cook 47 times. The fourth, fifth and sixth ascents of Tasman were all via the new routes, as if testing the proposition that the southern ridge was the easiest way to the summit. In 1927 Harold Porter and Marcel Kurz climbed the southern arête and then headed out into unclimbed territory down the North Ridge. Porter wrote: 'it was draped with row upon row of gigantic leaning columns of porous ice, perforated by deeply cut funnels of almost circular section' – an apt description of a ridge festooned with giant sastrugi.

The pair made quick work of the whole climb, descending from Engineer Col (named after Porter – who was an engineer) to

The East Face of Mt Tasman at dawn, with the Silberhorn Ridge on the left and Syme Ridge on the right. (Photo: Craig Potton)

the Grand Plateau and the comfort of Haast Hut – a luxury their predecessors had had to forego as the hut was completed only in 1917. Porter and Kurz were both Europeans, seasoned in the Swiss Alps, and confirmed Fitzgerald's prediction of cramponned ascents. Their climb took only seven hours and showed that marathon step-cutting efforts, awesome though they might be, were over. In a way, this introduction of new equipment also made the mountains more accessible, and proved a stimulus to the growth of the sport of mountaineering in the 1930s.

Throughout New Zealand in the 1920s there was a growing interest in outdoor recreation. As early as 1914 the New Zealand Alpine Club, founded in 1891, had been revived after being in recess for nearly 20 years. Restricted by stringent and rather exclu-sive membership rules, however, it remained a limited force until regional branches were created in the 1930s. Just as significant were tramping clubs. At a time when transport was limited and expen-sive, the club system provided the means for large numbers of young, less well off but strongly motivated climbers to get to the moun-tains. By the late 1920s the first of a new breed arrived in the Aoraki/ Mount Cook district.

Initially there was a considerable gap between the technical ability of the guides and the group of fledgling amateurs. Almost all of the early ascents of Tasman were led by guides. The sixth ascent was comprised entirely of guides; Jack Cox, Joe Fleurty and Jack Pope took time off from a hut-stocking trip on the Fox Gla-cier (Te Moeka o Tuawe) to make the first ascent of Tasman from

Harry Ayres (left) and Mick Bowie on the summit, 1954.
(Photo: Aoraki/Mount Cook National Park)

the west, via the North Ridge, the route descended by Porter and Kurz. Their employers, Peter and Alec Graham, who now ran the hotel at Franz Josef had encouraged them to play hookey, both from their love of the mountain and a desire to ensure that Franz Josef guides beat the Sullivan-employed guides from Fox Glacier township. For Cox, Fleurty and Pope, Tasman was a peak they had set their hearts on. For Fleurty especially, as a Poutini Ngai Tahu Maori from the West Coast, this mountain was a special challenge that he had wanted to test for years.

It was the fifth ascent however, which showed the growing power of amateur climbers. In January 1931 Rod Syme and Dan Bryant tackled the arête on the right side of the East Face of Tasman. The pair were well trained on the icy slopes of Mt Taranaki and made quick time up this beautiful rib of curving ice. They were on top by 9.30 a.m. and made a fast descent to the Fox Glacier névé over Mt Lendenfeld, and then crossed Pioneer Pass to return to Haast Hut by 5.30 p.m. Their route, now known as Syme Ridge, is one of the country's classic ice climbs.

By 1938 amateur climbs of the bigger routes in the area be-

came the norm, rather than guided ones. In 1940 Harry Stevenson and Doug Dick, both later presidents of the New Zealand Alpine Club, climbed Tasman via Syme Ridge and set out west along the giant sweep of the ridge connecting Tasman with Mt Torres. With doubts about the length of the route, the pair opted for an escape down the enormous sweeping snowslope on the West Face. At first they cut carefully down but their progress was so slow that they were forced to a more unorthodox technique. Stevenson wrote:

One man anchored firmly and the other man throwing all his weight on the pick end of the axe, commenced to slide down, but was unable to control himself, so had to be abruptly stopped by the man anchoring.

In this manner they reached the Fox Glacier névé and the prospect of a slog under a merciless sun in soft wet snow to Pioneer Pass and thence, after a bivouac, to Haast Hut. The route they started, the West Ridge, was finally traversed in January 1951 by Neil Hamilton, Les Cleveland and John Lange. They climbed Tasman via the North Ridge and then ventured out along the West Ridge, having the clear psychological advantage over previous parties of getting nearer rather than further from home, as they had built a snow cave 10 days earlier on Katies Col at the foot of Mt Torres. They found a good route down the rocks to the col between Tasman and Mt Torres. From here there were hours of solid climbing to the summit of Mt Torres. Les Cleveland commented:

Sometimes crampons could be scuffled into the crest; at other times a tricky crab-like sidling was needed. For a while we would descend a foot or so on one side or the other. Then perhaps we would use the ridge as a handrail while steps were being kicked.

From Torres they were on known ground and they reached their snow cave after a 21^1/$_2$ hour day, having completed one of the longer and more serious ridge traverses in New Zealand.

Neil Hamilton was to leave his mark on another climb on Tasman apart from the Torres Ridge. And this new climb was an important milestone in New Zealand mountaineering development. Rising onto the north shoulder of Mt Tasman from the Fox Glacier

Mt Tasman from the Fox Glacier. The three peaks of Mt Haast on left; Mt Lendenfeld at centre; and Mt Tasman on the right with the Heemskirk Face, North Rib, Abel Janszoon Face and West Ridge. (Photo: Nick Groves)

ment. They zigzagged slowly up the lower rocks of the buttress and bivouacked at about two-thirds height, having first reconnoitred the way ahead. Next morning they tackled the crux of the climb, a steep rock slab. Hamilton described it in the *New Zealand Alpine Journal*, 'the cracks provided excellent holds and with the safeguard of a few slings and running belays, I found it was not impossible'.

Maybe, but subsequent parties to climb the route have looked up at the lone rusting piton, and opted to traverse out left on snow and ice, an alternative noted but rejected by Hamilton. With some steep ice climbing between bulges, Hamilton and Berry completed their climb. While perhaps not an excessively difficult route, it was audacious in concept and certainly well ahead of its time.

With the West Buttress route climbed, there remained one last unclimbed ridge on Mt Tasman, an ice rib running from the remote Balfour Glacier to high onto the West Ridge. It was climbed on New Year's Day, 1959, by Wally Romanes, John Harrison, Brian Hearfield and Jim Wilson:

Of the three ice bulges we had reckoned with, one only gave difficulty and Wally led that very competently. This was before the Chouinard axe and before we got with front-point crampons, so we used to cut steps up such ice problems in those days, very safe. Jim Wilson

It was inevitable that in time New Zealand climbers would follow the European trend and move onto the faces. There were factors which had delayed this, not the least being the presence of still virgin ridges and the objective danger of many of the face climbs. It was the combination of New Zealanders returning from overseas and visiting climbers, bringing with them front-point crampons, ice pitons and a mental approach untouched by prevailing tenets of safe climbing, which heralded the breakthrough.

Tasman's East Face was first to succumb. In December 1936 John Pascoe and David and Duncan Hall had descended the greater part of the face when retreating from under the summit, preferring that alternative to a traverse back onto Syme Ridge. But that was a far cry from deliberately setting out to climb the face. In January 1960 for the German Eberhard von Terzi and Austrian Hans Leitner,

Mt Tasman from the Balfour Glacier showing the Hidden Face (centre), Balfour Rib and, in profile, the Balfour Face. (Photo: Craig Potton)

névé is a steep 500-metre rock buttress festooned with ice in its upper section. This obvious feature was investigated without success as early as 1935 by Jack Cox, Bill Fraser and 61-year-old pioneer Canon H E Newton. In December 1955 Hamilton and Alan Berry attacked the climb armed with rock pitons and bivouac equip-

the aim was no less than the *direttissima*. They first had to negotiate the maze of crevasses and seracs known as the Mad Mile, an area notorious for its avalanche danger, 'we could compare ourselves with ants in a freshly ploughed field'. Above the Mad Mile they continued up the broken face to the left of Syme Ridge and, with some assistance from ice pitons, pulled themselves over an ice lip and emerged only a few metres from the summit. They descended to Haast Hut, their fast time (six hours to the summit) for the climb being attributable in great measure to perfect teamwork and the use of front-point crampons.

Routes of equivalent difficulty had been climbed in the European Alps at least 30 years before, so the historical significance of these routes on Tasman derives more from their place as harbingers of a new era in the Southern Alps; within two decades the standard of the hardest New Zealand face climbs would equal their European equivalents.

There are three other faces on Tasman apart from the East Face; all of them, the Heemskirk, the Abel Janszoon and the Balfour, are on the western side of the mountain. The Heemskirk is really a flank rather than a face. It was climbed in 1972 by Wayne McIlraith and Maurice Conway and is now an admirable steep alternative route to the North Shoulder.

The Abel Janszoon Face is a neglected area. It lies on the sunny side of the mountain between the Torres Ridge and the West Buttress. Apart from the slope descended by Stevenson and Dick in 1940, only five separate climbs have been done on the face to date. A rib left of the Stevenson-Dick route was climbed in January 1969 by Murray Jones and George Harris which, while lacking technical difficulty, was serious and committing and, in Jones's words, 'a climb not to be recommended except for those who prefer giving the mountain a chance'.

Immediately to its left 'Nipple Rib', climbed in February 1982 by Phil Grover and John Nankervis, rises to a peaklet high on the West Ridge, has better rock and involved virtually no risk of baptism by rockfall from the couloir. On the northern side of the tot-

Abel Janszoon Face of Mt Tasman, with the North Face of Mt Torres on right. (Photo: Craig Potton)

tering central seracs Murray Jones and Merv English put up a line in December 1977, following ice slopes to a fierce finish through the ice flutings to the North Ridge 200 metres from the ice summit. In March 1983 Dave Bamford and John Nankervis climbed 'White Jasmine' on the left side of the Face which, from a first pitch in common with the Jones-English line, follows devious ice leads through a succession of rock bands to the ice cliffs immediately beneath the North Shoulder. Further left again, next to the North Buttress, is a major zigzag buttress capped by steep ice. This route, known now as 'Centurion', was climbed first in winter 1994 by Dave Crow, Andy Macfarlane and Jon Taylor, with two bivouacs. A later ascent in 2000 by David Hiddleston and Dave Vass added a direct variation up on the upper buttress. Being fairly close to Pioneer Hut, this promises to be a 'hard man's' classic.

Of Tasman's faces however, the glamour attractions lie in the Balfour Glacier. The Balfour Face with steep rock merging into intimidating bulging ice requires great commitment, and, tucked away round the corner, lies the Hidden Face. Here are rock ribs and gullies like prison bars and, above, yet more bulging ice. Access to them is serious and even on top the difficulties do not relent; no

Near the summit of Mt Silberhorn with the Grand Plateau 1,200 metres below and the Tasman Glacier beyond.
(Photo: Gottlieb Braun-Elwert/Hedgehog House)

descent of Tasman is ever a picnic!

With the surge in New Zealand climbing standards in the early 1970s the Balfour Face became *the* great challenge. In November 1971 the forceful Bill Denz, Bryan Pooley and Kevin Carroll, armed with new curved pickaxes, went onto the face. Denz wrote:

Round one terminated at the top of the Silberhorn but round two saw us on the wall itself and life at the sharp end. Pooley and I swung leads until on the fourth, through inexperience, I dropped a crampon. I took a 20 metre screamer while leading in one crampon up progressively icier ground. Pooley took over leading and shot up the right-tending ice ramps at the top of the rock instead of heading left of the ice bulges. We hit hard blue ice which we declined to climb and traversed right over the ground through which Strang and Wayatt later climbed. By now we were in a whiteout and opted for a retreat. The two-roped rappel landed us on a crisp 45° snow ledge ... This sortie was wild enough to scatter the team for a while. Bryan and I regrouped in Christchurch when we heard on the radio that George Harris and Chris Timms were on the Balfour Face. And then the weather socked in. I thought the odds of their having done the Face were about 50/50.

The storm put paid to Harris and Timms's chances, and so Denz and Pooley returned to the attack. Denz continues:

We got to the top of Silberhorn from Plateau Hut in 2 hours 40 minutes and started on the Balfour Face at about 6 a.m. Our previous wild attempt had given us the necessary experience to execute the first ascent safely and within 10 hours. We arrived back at the Plateau Hut at 8 p.m., tired but immensely satisfied.

The Balfour Face is now the ice climbers' *pièce de résistance*. There are at least four separate routes, each less than 100 metres apart, and it has been climbed solo at least three times. And it has been climbed in winter. The winter first ascent was again done by Denz. In a spur of the moment decision he and Phil Herron left their houses in Dunedin in mid June 1975, drove straight to Ball Hut, walked up to the Grand Plateau Hut (borrowing hut sleeping bags on the way) and then climbed over Silberhorn. They bivouacked the night in the middle of the face. Temperatures plummeted

to minus 25°C. Their waterbottles froze, and, for the next day and a half, they were without water. Added complications were ice axe breakages on the hard green ice. They reached the summit early on the second day but were faced with a descent on iron-hard green ice down the South Ridge and yet another bivouac before reaching the safety of Plateau Hut. This climb stands as one of the most daring in New Zealand in the 1970s, combining as it did remoteness, technical difficulty, poor conditions and cold.

The Hidden Face has not attracted the same amount of attention as the Balfour Face – perhaps because it is tucked away and not so visible, and perhaps because it is even more remote. There are nevertheless four routes. Noel Sissons and John Fantini climbed an obvious buttress in the middle of the face in 1975. Then Noel, with Greg Mortimer climbed an ice gully line alongside in 1979. The two hardest lines however, lie further left again, the first, the 'direct', was climbed by Guy Halliburton and Alan Wood in 1982. The second, just to the left beside the 'direct', was climbed by Brian Alder and Dave Vass in September 1989. Its name was 'Hippo takes a holiday'. It was no holiday.

It is fair to say that many of the major challenges in climbing Tasman have been met. There are still new lines to be climbed on the Abel Janszoon Face, and certainly there are new variations and new styles. With such slender arêtes and plummeting faces it is appropriate that New Zealand ice climbing should have been so positively reflected, if not influenced by, achievements on Mt Tasman. The spotlight may have moved elsewhere in terms of purely technical difficulty. But for those content just to climb this superb mountain it will always be, in the parlance of an earlier generation, a serious expedition.

Aerial view of Mt Tasman from the south showing the Torres Tasman Ridge on left, Hidden Face, Balfour Rib, Balfour Face and Silberhorn Ridge on right. (Photo: Rob Brown)

Labels on image: LENDENFELD, TASMAN, TORRES, WEST BUTTRESS, ABEL JANSON, HEEMSKIRK, THE BUTTRESS

(Photo: Nick Groves)

MT TASMAN
Classic Route: Lendenfeld–Tasman–Torres Traverse

Access: This climb is usually begun from the Pioneer Hut situated on the Pioneer Ridge on the Fox Glacier névé. From the hut it takes one hour to under Mt Haast if the climb is being done from Mt Lendenfeld or one and a half hours to Katies Col if the climb is being done from Mt Torres.

The Climb: Climb up the glacier (crevasses may necessitate careful route finding) to Marcel Col. From the col to the summit of Mt Lendenfeld and on down to Engineer Col is a straightforward snow and ice climb. Above Engineer Col the route tends left towards the top of Syme Ridge on the east and then to the North Shoulder. Ice changes can make the lower part of the route icecliff-threatened but conditions change from year to year. Beyond the North Shoulder a narrow ice ridge leads up to the summit of Mt Tasman.

The route from the summit follows the West Ridge to Mt Torres. The ridge is broad at first and then narrows, before dropping steeply down a rock rib to the Torres-Tasman Col. The route over Mt Torres involves climbing a snow and ice ridge with frequent rock steps. The descent from Mt Torres is a long rock ridge interspersed with snow ridges. Three quarters of a kilometre down it is wise to descend off the ridge to the west down a snow rib and onto a basin above the Balfour Glacier and then traverse around to Katies Col.

First Ascent: Les Cleveland, Neil Hamilton, John Lange: 6 January 1951

Grade 4

MT HICKS

One of New Zealand's more unobtrusive mountains is Mt Hicks. Lying hard under the western side of Aoraki/Mt Cook, Hicks is difficult to distinguish from either the west or east coasts. It is only when you climb higher on some of the southern ranges that the true size of this mountain becomes apparent, a stepping stone to nearby Aoraki/Mt Cook.

Mt Hicks is shaped like a half dome. The La Perouse and Hooker glaciers have carved away both the north and south sides of the mountain, leaving on the north an 800 metre face of solid red sandstone, and on the south a 600 metre precipice of ice and rock (of dubious quality) capped by an extensive icecliff. Only to the west and east are there ridges, and the eastern one is accessible only by climbing over the 3,443 metre high Mt Dampier. Thus, from all directions Mt Hicks presents a formidable mountaineering challenge. It is probably the hardest of peaks to climb in the Aoraki/Mt Cook district and, as an unfortunate death toll shows, it is a difficult peak to get down from.

Mt Hicks is named after Zachary Hicks, second-in-command on Captain Cook's first expedition to New Zealand in 1769. The mountain was originally named St. David's Dome by Thomas Broderick during his survey in 1891. St. David's Dome is a much more apt description of the peak, and still favoured by many. The change of name to Mt Hicks was decreed by the New Zealand Geographic Board, however, to conform with the navigator names of other major peaks in the Aoraki/Mt Cook district. George Roberts

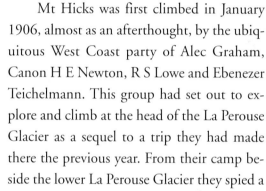

who was responsible for the West Coast survey and triangulation in the 1880s, is probably the person responsible for naming the mountain.

Mt Hicks was first climbed in January 1906, almost as an afterthought, by the ubiquitous West Coast party of Alec Graham, Canon H E Newton, R S Lowe and Ebenezer Teichelmann. This group had set out to explore and climb at the head of the La Perouse Glacier as a sequel to a trip they had made there the previous year. From their camp beside the lower La Perouse Glacier they spied a rock ridge running up from the La Perouse to the summit of Hicks. This proved a feasible route of ascent. Although steep in its upper section, the ridge was composed of firm red rock and took them without too much difficulty to a summit ridge, where only a short 30 metre wall provided any difficulties on the way. Their route, the West Ridge, was used by subsequent parties in the 1920s and 1930s approaching the mountain from the east via the Hooker Glacier, Harper Saddle and a short scramble up a rock face onto the ridge.

The other obvious approach to the summit of Mt Hicks is along the ridge from Mt Dampier. This ridge, however, is nowhere under 3,000 metres in altitude for its entire length, and involves climbing over Mt Dampier – not an easy proposition. Nevertheless the ridge saw many attempts, from as early as 1910 when the Graham brothers and Lawrence Earle contemplated attacking it from the upper Hooker Glacier, to the early 1930s when Harold

Left: Empress Hut and the South Face of Mt Hicks. (Photo: Bill King)
Above: South Face of Mt Hicks with the Left and Right Buttresses prominent. (Photo: Nick Groves/Hedgehog House)

Leading up steep ice on 'Heaven's Door', South Face of Mt Hicks.
(Photo: Kynan Bazley)

Porter twice failed with Vic Williams and, later, Jack Pope to complete the traverse from Hicks and back. Finally, in 1938, Jack Cox and Syd Brookes guided Marjorie Edgar Jones up Mt Dampier from the east and then completed the climb out along to Hicks, undertaking a forced night out lashed to rocks high on the West Ridge.

Nowadays Mt Hicks is regarded as one of New Zealand's most formidable peaks. The early climbers may not have been unanimous about this, but sometime early in the 1940s the mountain underwent a dramatic change. In 1946 two young students, George Lowe (later to make his name on Mt Everest) and Geoff Milne crossed Harper Saddle to climb the West Ridge. Ignorant of details of the route, they found the climb a lot harder than they were led to believe. There was a steep snowslope, under fire constantly from rockfall peeling off a huge slab of rotten rock above. Further up they found a narrow gully with some difficult rock steps, and no sign of enjoyable rock scrambling. Only above here did they encounter the familiar summit ridge with its 30 metre wall of solid red rock. The difficulty of the climb impressed the pair, as it did others who followed soon after. Mick Bowie, the Chief Guide at the Hermitage, ribbed the returning climbers, describing the route from his pre-war experience as 'an easy day'. In order to prove his point to the youngsters Bowie took some clients up the Hooker Glacier to do the route. From Harper Saddle he saw to his amazement that a huge section of the western side of the mountain had fallen away, destroying most of the West Ridge. Bowie climbed the route however, now used as the standard way up the mountain and called the Curtain Route. He confirmed that it was not an 'easy day'.

Bowie's revised judgement of the mountain has unfortunately proved tragically correct. The Curtain Route is subject to rockfall and icefall, is fully exposed to westerly storms, and for most parties entails a number of long rappels. In January 1981 Noel Sissons and Mary Atkinson, having climbed the South Face, were caught descending the Curtain Route in a storm which grew to frightening proportions. Ice sheathed the mountain, and hurricane force winds whipped the area for days. Noel and Mary's bodies were found a week later close together lashed on a rappel rope. Three years later, one of New Zealand's best rock climbers, Graeme Aimer, having also climbed the South Face, fell while rappelling down the Curtain Route at night.

Ridges on mountains provide the most obvious way to their summits. But for those seeking innovation, new challenges lie in the unclimbed and, in particular, in the face routes. There were new challenges aplenty on Mt Hicks. Its South Face is clearly visible from the Hermitage Hotel. The face's two prominent rock buttresses and frequent heavy coatings of ice are designed to repel, and yet paradoxically attract, the hardcore mountaineer. Less well known is the challenge of the North Face, larger, steeper and more friendly than the South Face, rising in splendid isolation above the La Perouse Glacier névé. For these reasons Mt Hicks always attracts top-class climbers. The list of first ascensionists of the face routes reads like Who's Who of New Zealand mountaineering. Harry Ayres and Oscar Coberger ventured out onto the edge of the South Face when they climbed the Main Divide route in 1951. David Elphick and Barry Smith climbed the top half of a buttress on the left of the North Face in 1957. The most prominent of the South Face routes, the Left Buttress fell to Murray Jones and Graeme Dingle in 1970. There are three names however, who feature above all others in the list of climbers. The first is Bill Denz, the second, Nick Cradock and the third, Bill McLeod.

Denz left his imprint on almost all of New Zealand's great mountains, but none more so than on Mt Hicks. It was the scene of some of his greatest triumphs in a career sprinkled with great climbs. His first effort was the Central Gullies route on the South Face, in its time one of the plum 'last great problems'. The competition to make a first ascent of this route was fierce and Denz naturally wanted a piece of the action. Another contender was Peter Gough. In November 1972 Denz teamed up with Swiss climber Etienne Kummer (later killed on the Dru in the Swiss Alps). De-

The superb rock architecture of the North Face of Hicks rising abruptly above the névé of the La Perouse Glacier. (Photo: Shaun Barnett/Black Robin Photography)

parting from the Hermitage late one afternoon, Denz cheekily wished Gough well and suggested he catch them up and come along. Furious at the thought of being left behind, Gough took Denz at this word.

I caught Bill Denz up at Hooker Hut where he had spent the night. 'Fantastic to see you', Bill said, 'you're just in time to come with us on the South Face. Who are you with?' 'Er, you!' I replied. This was a bit of a shock for Bill.

After some fast-talking by Gough, the climbers went onto the route as a threesome. Their line entailed some hair-raising leads by Denz on steep thin ice, accompanied by breakages of supposedly unbreakable ice axes and crampons. Finally, on dusk and in a snowstorm, they were forced to bivouac after some desperate climbing had failed to break through the summit icecliffs. Only in the morning, after a night in a coffin-like slot hacked in the summit icefields, could they find an easier alternative through the cliffs.

The Central Gullies was Denz's first new climb on Hicks. In the next ten years he claimed three more, two on the South Face and one on the North.

His North Face route was intended as a consolation prize for failing to make the first winter ascent of the South Face. This time he teamed up with Murray Judge and Phil Herron. Judge, with his technical brilliance, and Herron, with his unquenchable enthusiasm, complemented Denz's single-minded drive. They made the ascent of the Central Buttress on the North Face over two days. It was a superb climb, following a natural corner straight up a huge buttress of coarse red sandstone. Far from being a consolation prize, it is one of the best rock climbs in the Mt Cook district.

Denz's third route was on the South Face in 1975, again with Judge and Herron. They set out to tackle what they felt was one of the hardest lines they could find on the mountain, just left of the Left Buttress. On the second rope length they encountered a 30 metre free-standing ice pillar, which Denz led by leapfrogging his ice screws one above the other. Above the ice column they moved up a steep gully system beside the Left Buttress to the base of a prominent twin ice gully known as the Gunbarrels. In the dying twilight, Denz forced his way up the final pitch, in constant fear of falling off. His frequent yells of fear scared his companions witless, linked as they were to a poor belay and shaky ice protection. That night they bivouacked on a 50° ice slope and the following day climbed the easier-angled icefield to complete the climb by mid morning. The bottom section was not repeated till November 1998 when it was climbed without aid by Al Uren and Julian White. Unfortunately a large rockfall removed this section in June 1999!

Denz's final route on Mt Hicks was up the right of the Left Buttress on the South Face. He did it in 1981 with Nigel Perry in a swift no-nonsense single push. It marked the maturity that Denz's climbing had reached. He had never been totally satisfied with his earlier routes. Climbing as a group of three had been unwieldy, and Denz felt he had not executed the climbs as well as he could. Nevertheless, who can deny that making the first ascent of the best line of the North Face, in winter, or deliberately taking on the best unclimbed line on the South Face, in winter, did not lack a style of its own.

The second person to leave a major impression on routes on Mt Hicks was Nick Cradock. Unlike Denz, who tended to go for new routes immediately (why waste time with something done before), Cradock served a kind of apprenticeship. In 1975 and 1976 he climbed the North Buttress beside the North Face and the Central Buttress on the North Face. Then, in 1978, he and Nick Kagan established a new direct start to the Left Buttress on the South Face. There followed two innovative routes on the South Face with American climber Tobin Sorensen. Together in 1979 they did the Curver line just left of the Denz/Herron/Judge route in a mere eight hours. It was a style of climbing Denz alluded to. Two days later, the pair did an even better climb. Starting up a pillar of ice beneath the Left Buttress, Sorensen led some exceptionally fierce ice gullies with minimal protection. A committed Christian, Sorensen sometimes commented wryly that he needed no protection because he had 'higher help'. Whatever, the two climbers blitzed

Approaching the summit of Hicks from the west, with the Tasman Sea shining 3,000 metres below. (Photo: Nick Groves/Hedgehog House)

one of the best routes on the South Face in another amazing eight hour effort. At half height they encountered the Gunbarrel gullies but this hardly slowed them. The route, the Yankee-Kiwi couloir, was a real *tour de force*.

After the Yankee-Kiwi couloir, Cradock returned to Hicks again and again. In 1981 he and Neal Whiston climbed the Central Gullies on the South Face. In 1985 he made the first guided ascent of the Left Buttress on the South Face. Early in the following summer, he and Kevin Boekholt tackled a thin ice ribbon on the right side of the Central Gullies. This route had been climbed the previous year by Kim Logan and Pete Sinclair and had involved some aid climbing on ice.

Mt Hicks from the west, with the Curtain Route at left, the South Face to its right, and Mt Dampier behind. (Photo: Colin Monteath/Hedgehog House)

Cradock and Boekholt eliminated the aid, straightened the route out at the top, and then descended the Right Buttress. Cradock felt Logan had failed to complete the line properly, and therefore wanted to name the climb Logan's Retreat. The editor of the *Mount Cook Guidebook*, unwilling to offend Logan's feelings, named the route Logan's Run.

Cradock's final route was on the North Face. Between the Central and Left Buttress is an 800 metre gully of rotten black argillite rock – a place rock climbers would avoid like the plague. In most winters however, there is ice in the gully. In July 1986 Cradock and Guy Cotter ventured round into the La Perouse névé and headed up the gully. The climb, named Weeping Gash, took two days and involved some of the steepest ice Cradock had encountered. This was remarkable indeed for someone who had already encountered some of the steepest ice imaginable.

The third name associated with Mt Hicks was Bill McLeod. He was someone who dedicated himself to climbing with single-minded zeal. Reportedly he would return from climbs, not to relax and go to the pub, but return to his camp and do sets of press-ups and pull-ups. In 1985 he climbed the Curtain Route in winter. This signalled what was to come. Over the next eight years in winter he soloed the North Rib, the Yankee-Kiwi Couloir, and the South Face Left Buttress Direct. With partners he climbed in winter Logan's Run, the Left, Central and Right Buttresses on the North Face, and a new route on the right of the North Face. Viewed alongside his winter climbs on Aoraki/Mt Cook and a solo winter ascent of the Balfour Face of Mt Tasman, Bill McLeod stands as one of New Zealand's greatest climbers.

Mt Hicks is very much a mountaineer's mountain. The attraction of the peak has led to routes criss-crossing its most improbable parts. There are still unclimbed challenges though. The future will see new climbs and attempts to up the ante – winter solo ascents, speed ascents, multiple routes in one day. But whatever the approach, Mt Hicks will always deliver a fierce mountain experience.

LEFT BUTTRESS

RIGHT BUTTRESS

Photo: Shaun Barnett/Black Robin Photography

MT HICKS
Classic Route: North Face, Central Buttress

Access: From Mount Cook village it takes eight hours via the Hooker Glacier to reach Empress Hut at 2,500 metres at the head of the glacier. The glacier is heavily crevassed. From Empress Hut there is a complicated route to the bottom of the North Face of Mt Hicks. From the hut climb to Harper Saddle, descend the far side for 200 metres, keeping right, then ascend 150 metres onto a small névé under Mt Hicks. From the névé traverse below the North Rib of Mt Hicks and then descend 150 metres of rotten rock to the foot of the face. From Empress Hut it takes about four hours to reach the North Face.

The Climb: Start up a crack on a small block below the main buttress, then right and into the obvious groove that continues up the entire buttress. The route has a number of hard sections lower down (crux grade 15), and has a slight sting near the top. The rock is excellent. The climb usually involves some twenty-two rope lengths of climbing.

The descent from Mt Hicks is down the Curtain Route, a gully of snow or, in summer, rotten rock. A number of rappels are usually necessary. This is not a descent to be taken lightly.

First Ascent: Bill Denz, Phil Herron, Murray Judge: 3 June 1974

Grade 6

Moonrise over the top half of the 1,800 metre East Face of Mt Sefton. (Photo: Craig Potton)

MT SEFTON

Tourists visiting the Hermitage Hotel and Aoraki/Mount Cook village could be forgiven for believing that the highest mountain in New Zealand is Mt Sefton and not Aoraki/Mt Cook. Although Sefton is in fact almost 500 metres lower than Aoraki/Mt Cook, from the village it fills the whole western skyline. The base of the peak, only two kilometres away, rears up abruptly 2,000 metres in a serried row of ice cliffs and bluffs. The deep rumble of falling ice is a regular sound which echoes down the lower valleys.

Viewed from the east, the peak takes on the shape of a cresting wave, its long south ridge representing the tail and the steep east ridge the face of the wave. When viewed from the north or south, however, it resembles a sharp pyramid, causing an early observer to describe the mountain as 'the Matterhorn of New Zealand'. From all directions, and most particularly from the east and south, it is a prominent landmark.

An early European visitor, John Turnbull Thomson, the surveyor of much of the southeast of New Zealand, bestowed the name of Captain Stokes on the mountain to commemorate the Captain's great coastal survey of New Zealand in 1849–51. Five years later Julius von Haast visited the area, ignored all the names that had come before, and named the mountain Sefton, after William Sefton Moorhouse, then Superintendent of the Canterbury Province, and as such responsible for Haast's employment as provincial geologist. It is hardly surprising that Thomson wrote to Haast mildly rebuk-

ing him for the liberties he had taken with earlier names. But Sefton it remained.

To the growing number of tourists visiting the glaciers of the Aoraki/Mt Cook district the view of the spectacular eastern face of Mt Sefton was a highlight. In 1884 a small accommodation house, the first Hermitage, was established on the grass flats of the Hooker Valley on the south side of the Mueller Glacier. From this 'rough cottage' the summit of Sefton could be seen rearing above. The manager of the Hermitage, Frank Huddleston, studied the mountain's features in detail, and began taking tourist walks onto the then level moraines of the Mueller Glacier (it has since wasted over 100 metres and retreated a kilometre). Huddleston also named the mountain's flanking glaciers, Te Wae Wae and Huddleston. For the first 10 years, however, no one was tempted onto the peak.

Sefton's first protagonists were an interesting pair. In late 1894, a young 23-year-old Englishman, Edward Fitzgerald, employed a world-famous Italian guide, Mattias Zurbriggen, to accompany him on an exploring holiday to New Zealand. Fitzgerald's intention was to climb the highest peaks, especially Aoraki/Mt Cook. That he was thwarted in his ambition by three young New Zealanders rankled with the brash, aristocratic Fitzgerald. In a fit of pique he refused to recognise the Aoraki/Mt Cook climb as a worthy objective, even though in fact the New Zealanders' route had turned out to be a major mountaineering achievement. To salve his ego,

Mt Sefton from the north, with the east ridge dividing sunshine from shade. (Photo: Lionel Clay/Hedgehog House)

Looking from Mueller Hut at the South Ridge on the left, East Face, and East Ridge on the right.
(Photo: Colin Monteath/Hedgehog House)

Fitzgerald turned his attentions to Sefton, declaring, 'I was determined, come what might, I would not leave New Zealand as long as this peak remained unclimbed by me'.

It was a boast that nearly proved truer than Fitzgerald meant. Between January and February, Fitzgerald and Zurbriggen made several attempts on the mountain, establishing a campsite on a spur beside the Te Wae Wae Glacier at 1,600 metres. To reach their campsite, they were helped by Jack Clarke, a young 19-year-old who had been one of the three to beat Fitzgerald to Aoraki/Mt Cook. Fitzgerald employed the young Clarke as a porter, and took every opportunity to disparage the youngster, despite the fact that he was an able climber and later became one of New Zealand's most famous guides.

On the morning of the 14 February 1895, Fitzgerald and Zurbriggen left their camp, leaving Clarke behind. The pair, using crampons climbed to a broad, crevassed glacial shelf on the eastern face which they crossed and then ascended a snow rib leading to the col at the foot of the East Ridge, arriving at 6.30 a.m. From the col the ridge reared up. The bottom rocks were foully rotten but as they climbed the two found the nature of the rock improved. At about the halfway point, Zurbriggen, leading, was turning his attention to a short, steep section when Fitzgerald, who had just started up a wall below, fell unexpectedly. Zurbriggen was caught completely off guard as his hapless client tumbled towards the valley 2,000 metres below. Grabbing at the coils of the rope at his feet, Zurbriggen braced himself and single-handed stopped Fitzgerald's plunge. Zurbriggen desperately called down, first to ensure Fitzgerald was all right, and then to get him to secure himself and relieve the weight on Zurbriggen's arms. Once Fitzgerald had regained the rock, he shakily made his way up to Zurbriggen. To their horror, they found their climbing rope had almost completely cut through. A rest was called for while the pair calmed their shattered nerves.

It was only approximately 200 metres to the summit and it seemed unfortunate to turn back after the accident. So Fitzgerald and Zurbriggen pressed on to the flat section beneath the final rock buttress. This feature reared above them, likened in shape by a later party to a prow of a destroyer. The rock, however, was coated in icicles, so the two followed a steep shelf leading out over the North Face. Halfway across they took to the rocks and by 10.25 a.m. they had reached the summit. In celebration of victory, Zurbriggen produced a bottle of wine from his pack and he and Fitzgerald celebrated the first ascent.

All was not over however. They still had the descent. This they accomplished only with great care. At the spot where Fitzgerald had fallen, Zurbriggen used two great iron spikes to rappel from, the first use of pitons in New Zealand mountaineering. They slowly wended their way back across the shelf to their bivouac, arriving on dusk after a 20-hour trip to find Jack Clarke with a meal ready.

The climb received major publicity at the time. The experience moved Zurbriggen to declare:

Never, I can truly assert, have I found a mountain so absolutely dangerous as the peak we had just surmounted. It would be hard to find rocks in more frightful condition or crevasses more appalling to negotiate.

It was statements like these that caused the East Ridge to be looked on with awe by later generations of climbers. Over the next 45 years it was climbed only five times. To each party, its loose rock, exposed position and iced rocks presented a special challenge. Its reputation was undiminished when Peter Graham, the pre-eminent guide of his era, described it as the most demanding and potentially dangerous climb at Mt Cook. Each party that climbed it comprised skilled and experienced climbers. Only one group dismissed it more lightly. On 4 February 1925, Harold Porter and Frank Milne raced up the climb in six hours, and returned in four

Looking from the north summit to the south summit of Mt Sefton, with peaks of the central Southern Alps behind. (Photo: Gottlieb Braun-Elwert)

hours. Milne in particular was at the height of his powers, and had climbed the route nine years earlier with Samuel Turner and Peter Graham. He was an extraordinary mountaineer, one of the first in the country to train for his climbs. His gymnastic traversing around the walls of the old Hermitage amazed visiting tourists. Thus, on the East Ridge, he revelled on the rock, and led Porter, himself an able rock climber, at a cracking pace. On the way up they came across Zurbriggen's pitons:

[we] brought them down as trophies, one for Milne and one for me. What Z. wanted them for I can't understand; either he was terribly shaken by Fitzgerald's fall or there must have been a high wind, as the place he used them at, would not have deterred any competent lakeland climber.

Even so, later climbers continued to have difficulties on the climb. In 1937 Andy Jackson and David Lewis had an epic ascent, complete with Jackson taking a fall while leading a chimney, and suffering benightment on the Douglas Névé. In 1938 Jack Cox and Syd Brookes led Majorie Edgar Jones up the ridge, making the first ascent of the edge of the spectacular upper buttress. In 1949, Harry Ayres guided another party, and couldn't resist repeating this effort. Remarkably he climbed the prow solo, sending the rest of his party across the shelf. Although Ayres was to keep quiet about this breach of guiding principles for years, the challenge of the upper buttress made his climbing instinct win over his guiding responsibilities. Once on the top of the buttress, he had to wait over an hour, worrying where the rest of his group had got to. When they still hadn't appeared, Ayres proceeded to solo back down the buttress! Back at the shelf he spotted his two clients and second guide off-route on steep ground on the shelf. Speeding across, Ayres rejoined them, and they finally reached the summit via the top part of the West Ridge.

Despite its rich history, the East Ridge has, for some reason, never been a popular climb. It seems that the lower part of the ridge has collapsed on its northern side, exposing about 60 metres of rotten rock. This reputation has dogged the climb for years, but those who want to retrace the footsteps of New Zealand mountaineering history will discover that in fact the East Ridge is a premier climb.

The struggles of the early pioneers of the East Ridge led contemporaries to wonder whether there might not be an easier way onto Sefton's summit. The best hope seemed to lie from the West Coast. In 1895 explorer A P Harper discussed with Aoraki/Mt Cook first ascender Tom Fyfe, a possible approach from the southwest. Later, in 1909, a powerful party comprising Bernard Head, Lawrence Earle, Jack Clarke, Darby Thomson, Alec Graham and Peter Graham crossed from the Hermitage to the Douglas Glacier south of Sefton, but seeing from here the huge ice-cliffs of the Douglas Valley, decided that the Copland Valley to the northwest of the mountain could provide better access. Nine months later Head and Earle returned with Alec Graham and Jack Clarke. They crossed from the Hermitage over the Copland Pass and descended to the Douglas Rock bivouac. This was a well-used route crossing between Fox Glacier and the Hermitage which was rapidly becoming the most popular three-day tourist excursion over the Main Divide.

Douglas Rock was an enormous schist boulder sited on the bushline with a comfortable and sheltered space underneath. It had first been discovered by explorer Charles Douglas during his epic journey into the upper Copland Valley in the early 1890s. From the rock there were superb views of the upper valley, while behind, heavily vegetated bluffs and stream courses led to glaciers and snowfields high on the Sierra Range. Clarke and Graham believed if they could get up the bluffs, a route onto the range would open up. On 22 December 1909, the two guides and Head and Earle battled their way up through the scrub onto the ridge separating the Tekano Glacier and Scott's Creek and set up camp on snowgrass terraces. On 23 December they ascended the Tekano Glacier to a pass (later named Welcome Pass). Before them lay the vast expanse of the Douglas Névé and, to the east, a broad, easy West Ridge ran up to the summit of Sefton. They had discovered the 'easy' approach to the mountain – 'easy' in the sense that it was not a fierce, technical challenge. Later climbers were to refine the approach a little more by discovering a slightly less vegetated, lower approach up Scott's Creek. This route was descended by Darby Thomson, George Bannister and Samuel Turner on 17 March 1912. But the western approach to Sefton always is a long and complicated route, requiring good route finding, and not a little luck with the weather. The Douglas Névé is exposed to the west and any moisture rolling in from the Tasman Sea invariably brings thick mist and cloud, blocking views and hampering navigation. Many are the tales of bivouacs or nervous searches for Welcome Pass as parties descending the West Ridge seek the safety of the Copland Valley.

In March 1914 Canadian Otto Frind and his Austrian/Canadian guide Conrad Kain climbed a striking new route from the Mueller Glacier near the Hermitage onto Mt Thompson, a peak two kilometres south of Mt Sefton. Their climb lay from the Green Rock bivouac site, an area which, with dramatic down-shrinking of the Mueller Glacier, has now become inaccessible. In 1914 however, it was simply a matter of scrambling down a short moraine wall to the glacier. From here they climbed bluffs and onto a side glacier leading onto the Main Divide. To the north, they could see

A view of Mt Sefton's pyramid from the south – the vast Douglas Glacier and La Perouse on the left, Aoraki/Mt Cook behind (right), and the south face of Mt Thompson in the foreground. (Photo: Rob Brown/Hedgehog House)

reached the summit. They were also hampered by Frind's interest in photography. He insisted the party take his full plate camera, and stopped to compose 33 photographs! On their return they camped on Brunner Col, next day climbed Sharks Tooth, and were back at the Hermitage by late afternoon to celebrate.

Frind, Kain and Young's route remained neglected for years. Even when the South Ridge was climbed, the party chose the vastly longer, but less difficult approach via the Douglas Glacier. On 1 January 1948 Earle Riddiford, Bill Beaven, Jim MacFarlane and Norman Hardie climbed the ridge, avoiding two hard steps near the top. Just over 30 years later Stu Allan, Olly McCahon, Rob Rowlands and Brin Williman repeated the route exactly and climbed the steps. It was not until January 1973 that two Swiss climbers working at the Hermitage completed what Frind and Kain had originally wanted to do. Otto von Allmen and Hans Müller climbed from the Mueller Glacier to Brunner Col, raced up the South Ridge, and then descended the West Ridge and so into the Copland Valley to Douglas Rock – all in 19 hours, a remarkable *tour de force.*

On the far side of the South Ridge of Sefton is another feature of the mountain so large that the many decades of climbers and hikers following the track down the Copland Valley failed to recognise it for what it was. In 1963, however, a photograph taken from the nearby Strauchon Valley was published in the annual journal of the Canterbury Mountaineering Club. It showed a huge rib beginning just up the Copland Valley from the Douglas Rock Hut and rising 2,000 metres directly to the summit of Sefton. It was easy to see how it had not been obvious, for from below it takes the form of massive impossible-looking bluffs, while hanging glaciers either side seem to threaten the lower approaches.

The 1963 photograph did not pass unnoticed by the climbing community. In December 1964 Nick von Tunzelmann, Aat Vervoorn and Bruce Harrison were climbing in the Hooker Valley, and instead of returning down valley to the Hermitage decided to seek a more exciting route back via Baker Saddle which took them to the Strauchon Valley on the West Coast, and thence to the

Edward Fitzgerald (left), Mattias Zurbriggen and the old Hermitage, 1895.
(Photo: Kinsey Collection: Canterbury Museum)

the challenging stepped South Ridge leading north to Sefton. The view whet their appetites so on 22 March 1914 they returned with New Zealand guide Dick Young, intent on a new route on the mountain. They climbed from the Mueller to Brunner Col. Above, the South Ridge reared up but to their left was a narrow snow shelf which they knew would lead them round onto the Douglas Névé and the easier approach of the West Ridge. The Névé was badly broken, however, and it was not until late in the day that they

Copland Valley. On the way they obtained superb views of Sefton's rib, the North Ridge and, although they were aware of the route, the sight confirmed in their mind that they should give it a go.

In the early hours of a December morning the three left Douglas Rock and proceeded to get lost in the scrub. After blundering around for an hour and going back to the hut, they tried again at first light. The lower buttresses and bluffs proved easier than they expected and the three gained height rapidly. Above a long slope of scree, they headed up three rock buttresses. As they climbed unroped, this steep loose ground needed careful concentration. By mid-afternoon they had surmounted the three buttresses and reached a level ridge. Above lay an obstacle they thought would be the key to the climb. The icecap of Sefton rolled down across the rib forming an ice wall. For Vervoorn and Tunzelmann this was no great problem, but Harrison only had ten point crampons without front claws making climbing steep ice harder for him. In the event, however, the ice was soft, and protected by the rope from above, the three were able to scramble onto slightly easier angled snow. It was still a long slog up snow and ice to the junction with the West Ridge, and from here only a short distance to the summit.

The North Ridge ascent was a superb performance. Vervoorn, Tunzelmann and Harrison managed to descend to the Copland Valley that evening, despite being hampered by thick mist and setting off massive soft snow avalanches. Their route presented excellent climbing, but it was not until the late 1970s that it was recognised as the classic climb that it is. Indeed, in many ways, it is probably the most satisfying way for the competent climber to tackle Mt Sefton.

Apart from Sefton's ridges, the mountain has two significant faces. The North Face is a steep rock face, and is often heavily iced up. It was climbed by Steve Elder in November 1987 via a narrow ice gully which winds up the centre of the face. Sefton's other flank is the East Face, directly opposite the Hermitage Hotel. The prominent feature is a long row of ice cliffs two-thirds of the way up forming the edge of the Upper Shelf Glacier. The East Face is not spectacularly steep, but it is heavily-glaciated and the active rows of ice cliffs put much of its area off-limits to climbers who want to live long. There is a relatively safe area, however, lying up the bluffs

Ascending the East Ridge of Sefton in deteriorating weather.
(Photo: Colin Monteath/Hedgehog House)

above the Mueller Glacier and up between the left of the Upper Shelf Glacier and the tumbling ice fall descending from Tuckett Col on the right.

The first ascent of the East Face was made in January 1953, for its time, a bold undertaking. Bert Barley, Fred Edwards and Geoff Harrow had just completed a series of good climbs up the Hooker Valley, and were well on the way to climbing most of the 3,000 metre peaks. Bert Barley had spent a lot of time in the previous years working at the Hermitage and rebuilding the mountain huts of the region, and he had spent a great deal of his time reconnoitring the East Face. He realised the crux of the climb was to get onto the Upper Shelf Glacier. Above it a diagonal gully led up high onto the South Ridge. To reach the glacier the three climbers used the approach to the East Ridge across the Huddleston Glacier. Rather than ascend to Tuckett Col though, they cut across to a steep slope under the Shelf Glacier. In making the crossing, however, they were forced to sprint across an area strewn with debris of ice blocks which had fallen from threatening icecliffs under Tuckett Col. Putting some steep climbing behind them, Barley, Edwards and Harrow reached the Shelf Glacier and then cut their way up steep hard ice in the diagonal gully to reach the summit ridge.

Climbing the middle rock buttresses during an ascent of the 2,000 metre long North Ridge of Mt Sefton. (Photo: Bill King)

The Huddleston Glacier approach to the East Face was used a number of times over the next twenty years, but climbers usually missed the lower sections and traversed onto the Shelf Glacier from Tuckett Col. In 1963 Kobi Bosshard, Fritz Schaumberg and Mike Goldsmith climbed a steep new variation to the summit just to the south of the South Summit of Sefton. A vicious storm had developed as they were climbing making it impossible for them to cross the summit ridge, forcing them into an epic descent back down their line of ascent on the face. Another more spectacular variation up the summit wall was made in December 1967 by Pete Gough and George Harris. A thin ribbon of ice droops down between the North and South summits. Gough and Harris had ventured onto the face and encountered heavy soft snow. Their comparative inexperience had forced them to climb slowly. They arrived at the foot of the ice tongue late in the day, with the ice wet from the sun's rays, and threatening weather gathering to the west. With a certain sense of desperation Gough launched himself up the steep gully, realising that descent back down the face in the avalanche-threatening conditions would be an extremely unpleasant alternative. He struggled up the ice, but was eventually forced to take to rotten rock on its side. He placed a jamnut runner and climbed higher, placing a piton. A minute later Harris was startled by a cry as Gough fell through the air surrounded by flying rocks. The piton ripped out and it was only the jamnut that saved him. Although shaken, Gough returned to the attack and eventually made it to a reasonably secure stance 50 metres from the summit. It remained only for Harris to lead up the now semi-frozen ice to the ridge. In rather emotional language, Harris described their relieved embrace once they realised they were safe.

While all the early ascents of the East Face used the Huddleston Glacier route, it seemed obvious that there must be a route lying directly up the bluffs from the Mueller Glacier and connecting with the Barley/Edwards/Harrow line. This new approach was used by Ross Gooder, John Stanton and Murray Jones in January 1971. The climb was marked by controversy. Jones set off to climb the route alone, and, unknown to him, so did Stanton and Gooder. The meeting on the mountain was slightly less than cordial, with the taciturn Jones resenting what he saw as an intrusion by the other two. As a finale, however, all three gravitated towards the gully between the two summits where Pete Gough had had such troubles in 1967. Once there Jones realised that the difficulties would force him to join up with Stanton and Gooder. Differences forgotten, they climbed to the summit together. In January 1990 Peter Dickson chanced his arm by climbing the prominent rock buttress below the right side of the upper serac line. Although reputed to be fairly safe from the hourly icefalls of the seracs, the route's name perhaps hints at the possible perils. The route's name is 'For Whom the Bell Tolls'.

SEFTON

EAST RIDGE

WEST RIDGE

COPLAND VALLEY

Photo: Geoff Spearpoint

MT SEFTON
Classic Route: North Ridge

Access: From Mount Cook village walk up the Hooker Valley and cross the Copland Pass, descending the Copland Valley to Douglas Rock Hut. This usually takes at least eight hours. Alternatively, walk up the Copland Valley from SH 6, allowing eight hours to reach Douglas Rock Hut.

The Climb: Walk 30 minutes up the Copland Pass track from Douglas Rock and climb up scree and a snow slope below the Jasper Glacier (look out for avalanches). Then cut off the snow onto bluffs to the north. The bluffs give way to an easy angled scree, and then good climbing to the first of three large rock buttresses. Climb each buttress, staying near the crest where possible. The rock is variable and steep. If possible avoid belayed climbing as this will slow you down, but be careful! Above the buttresses the ridge flattens out and then merges with snow and ice below the summit. Climb a vague snow rib to reach an ice shelf just below the summit. Traverse right onto the upper slopes of the West Ridge.

Descend the West Ridge to Welcome Pass (it's the third major dip in the ridge). Below Welcome Pass traverse across the Tekano Glacier into the head of Scott's Creek. Scott's Creek leads down (via a waterfall, traversed on the true left) to Welcome Flat in the Copland Valley.

In order to complete this very long climb quickly, climbers need to be confident in climbing unroped on steep ground.

First Ascent: Bruce Harrison, Nick von Tunzelmann, Aat Vervoorn: 28 December 1964

Grade 3+

Straddling the beautiful red rock of the cheval section of the West Ridge of Malte Brun. (Photo: Rob Brown)

MALTE BRUN

If it can ever be said that a mountain is identified with one person's achievements, then that mountain is Malte Brun. And the person is Tom Fyfe. At the dawn of modern New Zealand mountaineering Tom Fyfe climbed Malte Brun alone. This might seem a rather insignificant event if it were not for the nature of the mountain. For Malte Brun is no easy walk up low-angle scree slopes. It is the highest point on the Malte Brun range, a group of mountains running 10 kilometres east of the Main Divide and including prominent peaks like Haeckel, Hamilton, Aiguilles Rouges, and Chudleigh. On either side of the range are the two longest glaciers in New Zealand, the Tasman and the Murchison. Malte Brun lies roughly in the middle of the range. On both sides it supports small glacier névés; on the east the Baker and on the west, the Bonney, which in turn feed the two large valley glaciers. The approaches to these névés are not immediately obvious, and above them the peak rises a further 500 metres. Above the Baker névé is an ice face; above the Bonney a series of rock ribs. On a remarkable, historic evening in March 1894, Fyfe, a young itinerant plumber from Timaru, lay in the rock bivouac at the foot of De La Beche Ridge and scribbled a note 'played a lone hand and won'. Fyfe had that day climbed the North Face of Malte Brun.

Fyfe's climb was not a random feat. He had planned it. In 1892, when working on a new extension to the old Hermitage cob accommodation house, he had fallen in love with the mountains. In the next three years he made frequent visits from Timaru, scrambling around the area. In 1893 he joined forces with the group of young climbers who had their sights on Aoraki/Mt Cook. By early 1894, Fyfe had a good understanding of the topography of the Aoraki/Mt Cook area – maps were very rudimentary – and had developed into a superb rock climber.

Peter Graham, the chief guide at the Hermitage from 1905–1922 said of Fyfe, 'I have always considered him the priest of early mountaineers and as a rock climber he was unsurpassed'.

On 6 March 1894 Fyfe walked from the small Ball Hut eight kilometres down valley to the bivouac rock at the foot of the De La Beche Ridge where the Rudolf Glacier joins the Tasman Glacier. To the east, three kilometres away, stood Malte Brun, its ramparts rising in the afternoon sun and reflecting the red-brown of its sandstone and argillite rock.

It is easy to assume that the peak's name derives from its colour. In fact it was named in 1862 by the ubiquitous geologist, Julius von Haast, after Victor Adolphe Malte-Brun, secretary general of the Geographical Society of Paris. Malte-Brun was a man that Haast, with his eye ever on approval from the European scientific establishment, was keen to flatter. And so it remained Malte Brun even though later generations have refined the name to a popular form: 'Malte'.

Haast seems to have been one of the first people to become aware of Malte Brun's prominence. From the lower Tasman Valley Malte Brun is hard to distinguish from its neighbours, and it is not

On the summit of Malte Brun. (Photo: Craig Potton)

Old Malte Brun Hut, 1912. Top, left–right: Jack Clarke, Freda du Faur, Jim Dennistoun, Alec Graham, George Bannister, Peter Graham; Bottom, left–right: Mary Ainsley, Barbara Dennistoun, Ada Julius, Hugh Chambers, George Dennistoun. (Photo: Riley Collection: Canterbury Museum)

visible from the West Coast or from the valleys to the north or south. It is only when climbing out of the Tasman Valley, up the Haast Ridge towards Mt Cook for example, that it reveals its true stature. In 1882 the Rev. W S Green wrote during the first attempt on Mt Cook:

One of the peaks of the Malte Brun chain was particularly striking, and every now and then either Kaufmann or Boss would give expression to their admiration of its bold outline, standing up like a pyramid of rock from the glaciers which clung to its flanks.

It was this pyramid which Fyfe was looking at on 6 March. By good fortune the aspect of Malte Brun he was viewing favoured Fyfe's climbing capabilities. It was predominantly rock, and remarkably solid rock by the standards of the rather questionable material elsewhere in the Aoraki/Mt Cook area. Malte Brun is composed of a series of large folds of argillite and sandstone. On its northern and western sides are numerous ribs and buttresses of solid red sandstone, and in the summer at least, little ice. The looser argillites and the heavier glaciation are found on the mountain's southern and eastern aspects.

Mountaineers are rather perverse people. They rise in the cold hard hours after midnight, not because they really want to, but in order to be up and moving before the day's warmth turns firm crampon-hard snow to slush, and before the sun's rays turn snowslopes into white furnaces. Fyfe rose early on the morning of 7 March, probably well before four o'clock. His breakfast would have been cold, or else cooked over a paraffin burner. The preparation can't have taken long because by 4.45 a.m. he was on his way. He would have had a simple short walk to the Tasman Glacier in 1894. In the ensuing years the glacier has melted down 100 metres, leaving a huge rotten moraine wall below the old De La Beche bivouac, and where Fyfe's bivouac rock once nestled in a cosy hollow, slumping of the moraine wall has left it perilously close to the edge. Modern climbers use a comfortable hut sited on solid rock 125 metres further up the ridge.

Above the Tasman Glacier, Fyfe chose a rather unusual route. The modern approaches to Malte Brun's northern side are up the short steep Malte Brun Glacier to gain the west ridge, or via the Turnbull Glacier to a small low pass onto the Bonney Glacier névé, above which are the north ridge and north face of the mountain. From where Fyfe left the Tasman Glacier, it would have seemed simplest to follow up the Turnbull Glacier. Instead he climbed the small peak on the north side of the glacier and then along a narrow rotten ridge until he reached the junction with the Bonney Glacier névé. In climbing up this route, Fyfe noted,

… for about 1000 ft there is a series of large 'terraces'. The base of this spur is very suitable for a bivouac, and firewood is obtainable in small quantities.

Four years later a hut was built on these terraces slightly down valley from where Fyfe climbed up. The site was chosen by T N Broderick, the pioneer surveyor of the Mount Cook district, as a suitable place for tourists visiting the upper Tasman Glacier. Set in attractive surroundings of shrubs and tussock grass, the hut made for a scenic and more comfortable site than the austere accommodation under the large rock across the valley at De La Beche Cor-

South Face of Malte Brun from the Beetham Valley, with the West Ridge on the left and South Ridge on the right. (Photo: David Chowdhury)

ner where Fyfe had spent the night. In those days, Malte Brun Hut was a comfortable four to five hours walk from Ball Hut. The walk became a popular attraction among the growing number of visitors to the Hermitage and provided regular work for the guides. Time took its toll with the original hut however, and in 1931 it was replaced by a larger building 150 metres south. This hut in turn was rebuilt in 1950. At the same time recession in the Tasman Glacier made the walk up from Ball Hut more and more onerous. Finally the terraces began to slump away and with the moraine wall steepening and creeping ominously close, in 1979 the Malte Brun Hut site was abandoned and a new structure built much further south and lower down the range in the Beetham Valley. This in turn was destroyed by an avalanche in the 1990s.

Tourist excursions to the Malte Brun Hut lay in Fyfe's guiding future. For the moment, standing on the col between the Turnbull and Bonney glaciers, he contemplated the hardest part of the climb. He had intended originally to climb the north ridge of the mountain. In his account he did not make it clear whether he meant the North East Ridge or the North Rib. It was probably the latter. In any event, a maze of crevasses put him off. The North Rib would have to wait until 1906 when it was climbed by Peter Graham and Henrik Sillem, and the North East Ridge until 1951 when Harry Ayres and Bruce Gillies reached it by traversing Mt Hamilton. Fyfe was reluctantly coming to the conclusion that he had failed. On looking at the mountain more closely however, he reasoned that the North Face directly opposite him might not be as bad as it looked.

My reason for thinking that this could be climbed was that it had exactly the same appearance as the final part of De La Beche, which Graham [George Graham - Fyfe's partner on Mt Cook the following year and no relation of Peter, of the guiding Graham family from the Franz Josef] and I had found comparatively easy.

Consequently, Fyfe set out across the Bonney to take a look. He was still worried about crevasses. At one point he collected a heavy stone for each hand to give him momentum to jump over a slot, and at a couple of other points he belayed himself with the rope to his ice axe while he tested the crevasse edges. It has to be remembered that Fyfe was still relatively inexperienced, particularly in snow and ice climbing. Also, he was without the modern climber's equipment of twelve point crampons, plastic boots and 40-metre-long nylon ropes. Fyfe had nailed boots, a short hemp rope, and a long alpenstock. He did, however, have one innovation modern climbers would recognise – a pair of rubber soled shoes:

But for these the peak would still be unclimbed. They seem to get a safe hold almost anywhere and on rock peaks the best climbers should go provided with one or more pairs.

Before he could use them however, he had to climb part way up a narrow 250-metre-long snow gully. As soon as he could Fyfe cut onto the rock because of stones falling down the gully. At this stage, he changed to rubber soled shoes. Fyfe was now in his element. In his own words, 'the variety and difficulty of this climb was enough to satisfy any lover of rock work'. Fyfe swarmed his way up the rock and at 12.40 p.m. reached the summit ridge. From here it was a matter of traversing a series of minor summits until he reached the highest point.

A bitterly cold wind was blowing up from the south to Fyfe's left. A snowslope plunged off down the east face. This side of the mountain was left untouched until the summer of 1952–53 when in quick succession a gully on the face just left of the East Rib was climbed by Bernie Gunn, Fred Hollows, Barrie Jackson and Gillian Soper, while a few days later the East Rib was ascended by Earle Riddiford, Bill Beaven, Ian Gibbs and Hugh Tyndale Biscoe. The central part of the East Face was climbed in 1978 by John Nankervis and Richard Hancock. Fyfe certainly would have given no thought to the East Face. The cold wind drove him back down the way he had come. He built a small rock cairn on one of the middle summits, leaving a bone-handled knife with his initial and a date scratched on the bone. Then, after a bite to eat, he began to carefully retrace his route down the North Face.

On the descent he tried to pick an easier route more towards the centre of the face, but ended up in difficulty. Twice he had to loop his rope over a rock and lower himself down. Finally, after some tricky manoeuvres Fyfe reached the head of a snow couloir, the foot of which he had used to start the climb. The snow was now softer but no sooner had he started kicking steps down than he heard the sound of rockfall. Looking up a cascade of boulders were pouring towards him. Fyfe saw little alternative but to trust himself to the wind and leap off, in a hope that he would beat the rocks to the bottom, that he would break no bones during his wild 250 metre slide, and that the snow at the bottom would be soft enough to slow him without fatal results.

The couloir was very steep, the snow hard, and by lying flat on my back, I simply went down as if flying through the air. The small schrunds I do not remember at all, for it was impossible to keep my eyes open.

Luck was with Fyfe that day and he lived to regain the rock bivouac at De La Beche Corner. Today climbers look at the gully and marvel at Fyfe's wild ride. Some have mistakenly believed that he flew down a prominent couloir further right on the face which joins the top of the West Ridge. In fact, Fyfe's gully was a smaller one, but as a memorial to the feat, the large gully is now known as Fyfe's Gut, a very unhealthy place on a warm afternoon when rockfall and soft snow slides combine and where more than one climber has suffered serious injury from rockfall.

A winter aspect of Mt Hamilton (left) and Malte Brun (right), with the North Face of Malte Brun rising above the Bonney Glacier. (Photo: Colin Monteath/Hedgehog House)

Fyfe's ascent was a feat of daring and courage. The route he climbed was not to prove a classic however. The North Rib and North Face has been climbed many times since, but today's climbers prefer another way to the summit, the classical West Ridge.

The West Ridge lies on the southern side of the North Face and divides the face from the mountain's southern flank which rises from the Beetham Valley and Malte Brun Pass. The ridge sweeps up above the Tasman in a 500 metre step before levelling out and then rising a final 200 metres to the summit. The first to climb the ridge were Peter Graham, Freda du Faur and Lawrence Earle. Graham had checked out the route during two earlier ascents on other routes – the North Rib with Sillem, and in 1909 when he climbed the shaly South Ridge with Claud MacDonald and second guide Jim Murphy. Graham was confident in the abilities of his two clients. Freda du Faur was a protégée of Graham's and a strong rock climber. Earle, a rather impetuous Englishman, had nevertheless proved himself on a number of climbs including the ridge on Aoraki/Mt Cook now named after him. In the event the climb proved relatively straightforward. It took the party six and a half hours to reach the summit. Graham wrote:

This route by the western arête was the third by which I'd climbed the mountain and I thought it the finest and most interesting.

The most exciting part was a narrow knife-edge known as the cheval, ascended by Graham and his party by sitting astride the ridge.

The East Face of Malte Brun, with the East Rib on the right.
(Photo: Colin Monteath/Hedgehog House)

In 1912 guide Jack Clarke and Hugh Chambers achieved a variation which wound its way up the Malte Brun Glacier and then up rock slabs onto the West Ridge just short of the cheval. This variation has proved to be the 'golden road' to the summit, enjoyed by all those who want a mountaineering challenge without the strain of severity or dangers of rock or icefall.

In 1980 a modern 30 bunk hut was built in the Beetham Valley, on a grass terrace beside the Beetham Stream, an hospitable and scenic little corner amongst a world of rock, ice and moraine. The hut gave easy access to the West Ridge of Malte Brun, and to Malte Brun Pass and the South Ridge. It also allowed access to the mountain's South Face, a cold and rather loose climb, but blessed with being the closest part of the mountain to Beetham Valley. The hut was destroyed by avalanche in 1995. Today's climbers of Malte Brun can either camp, or seek shelter under incipient bivouac rocks in the charms of the tussock of the lower Beetham Valley, or else chance their arm ascending the steep rubble moraine walls below the terraces of Turnbull and Malte Brun Glacier. In a way, nature is calling on modern climbers to accept a style of ascent, as Fyfe did in 1894.

MALTE BRUN

North Ridge, *West Ridge*, *Bonney Glacier* (labels on image)

Photo: Institute of Geological and Nuclear Sciences

MALTE BRUN
Classic Route: West Ridge Variant

Access: Starting from the Ball Hut road walk up the moraine wall track to Ball Shelter, then descend to the moraine-covered Ball Glacier. From here cross over to what remains of the white ice of the Hochstetter Glacier. Then cross the Tasman Glacier moraine onto the white ice of the Tasman Glacier and from here head up the glacier to opposite the Beetham Stream. Cut off the Tasman Glacier and follow a rough track up the south side of the stream to a wire bridge.

Alternatively, head further up the Tasman Glacier and up a steep rock gully onto old moraine terraces in the vicinity of the original Malte Brun Hut site below the Malte Brun Glacier. This route is subject to change due to moraine wall collapses.

The Climb: From the lower Beetham, cross the base of the West Ridge, northeast of the bridge and sidle around, gaining height to reach basins below the Malte Brun Glacier. Climb up the glacier. Near the top of the glacier climb right into one of a series of gullies onto a small snowfield and then up a short rock face onto the main ridge. Once on the ridge negotiate a narrow level section (The Cheval), and then on up 200 metres of rock to the summit.

Descend the same way, or traverse the mountain by descending the North Ridge to the Bonney Glacier, or the South Ridge (which has some steep rotten rock on it) to Malte Brun Pass.

First Ascent: Hugh Chambers, Jack Clarke: 7 February 1912

Grade 3-

MT ASPIRING

At the head of Hawea about 40 miles distant is a very lofty conical peak which I called Aspiring.

So reads the field book of surveyor John Turnbull Thomson under an entry dated 18 December 1857. Thomson, one of the first Europeans to explore Central Otago was recording his first sighting of the mountain that Maori had named Tititea, the glistening peak.

If any mountain deserves the description of elegant, then it is Aspiring. The peak rises as a giant white spire out of the great icefields of the Bonar, Therma and Volta glaciers. With no summit for over 50 kilometres to challenge it in height, Aspiring is the pre-eminent peak of southern New Zealand, rivalled in size only by the bulky 3,000 metre summits of the Aoraki/Mount Cook district, 180 kilometres north, none of which can surpass it for beauty of form.

Aspiring is best visualised as a four-sided pyramid, with ridges running southeast, southwest, northeast and northwest. Between each ridge, glaciers have cleanly carved faces to each of the four points of the compass. Resting 700 metres below the summit are, on the south and west the névé of the Bonar Glacier, on the north the Therma névé, and on the east the Volta névé. These three great glaciers drain into vast, dense forest and impenetrable gorges of the South Westland valleys of the Waipara and Waiatoto. In the east, the mountain stands over a kilometre back from the main divide and the walls rise from the gentler beech forest and grassy terraces of the east and west branches of the Matukituki River.

With such surrounds it is hardly surprising that visitors to the area never fail to be impressed by Aspiring. West Coast pioneer explorer Charlie Douglas made constant references to the peak in his diaries during his explorations of the Waipara and Waiatoto. He took pains to ensure he completed sketches of 'the splendid views' of Aspiring. From the east the 'silver cone' was held out to visitors as one of the landmarks of the Lake Wanaka and Lake Hawea districts.

Given its reputation, it was surprising that attempts to climb the peak came comparatively late. It was not until 1905 that West Coasters Ebenezer Teichelmann, Alec Graham and Dennis Nolan explored the northern approaches from the Waiatoto Valley, and mounted a serious attempt on the peak. After days of track cutting and packing stores, the trio reached the terminal of the Therma. A visit eighteen years earlier by Charlie Douglas described the rigours of the upper Waiatoto Valley:

Altogether this has been one of the roughest days travelling I have had for years, and no-one but a Lunatic will ever visit the Therma Glacier twice, unless a track is cut ...

Undeterred by bush, boulders and the weight of Teichelmann's full plate camera, Graham, Nolan and Teichelmann established a camp under a leaning rock near the glacier snout. To Graham, the

The beautiful pyramid of Mt Aspiring at sunset in winter. The classic South West Ridge on right, North West Ridge on left and the Bonar Glacier in the foreground. (Photo: Craig Potton) Above: Sunset on Mt Aspiring. (Photo: Craig Potton)

Summit of Aspiring, 1935: A S Ombler,
E O Dawson, W S Gilkison, R D Dick.
(Photo: H Stevenson)

first view of Aspiring was encouraging. He picked out a route onto the North West Ridge, which to him seemed to present no obvious difficulties. On 1 February they made their attempt on the peak. Distance and time were against them, however, and instead they climbed Glacier Dome, an easier and more accessible peak. From here, Graham again had a good view of his favoured route up the North West Ridge. But to his intense disappointment it was not to be. Teichelmann had commitments with his medical practice back in Hokitika, and he was concerned that with a long battle down the Waiatoto still ahead of them, they could easily be trapped by bad weather. He prevailed on Graham to head home, with the promise of another attempt in the years to come.

The following year Alec Graham indeed returned. But to his sorrow, it was without his friend Teichelmann. Instead, Graham received a letter from guide Jack Clarke asking him to accompany a party comprising himself, Clarke, Captain Bernard Head and Lawrence Earle to climb the mountain from the east via the Matukituki Valley. It seems likely that Graham accepted the offer rather reluctantly. He would have preferred to be with Teichelmann, and did not hold Head, and especially Earle, in very high regard. Earle had earned the generous-spirited West Coaster's contempt for selfish behaviour when he, Head, Alec and Peter Graham, Jack Clarke and Darby Thomson had been caught the previous summer on low rations in the upper Landsborough to the north:

Food by now was rather short, but I think Mr Earle was a bit better off for he carried some extracts in his rucksack and I noticed him enjoying them outside the tent from time to time.

In the event, Earle withdrew from the party, and so it was left to Graham, Clarke and Head to explore Aspiring from the east. Their first foray was up the East branch of the Matukituki. Here, however, they found huge cirque walls blocking them from the peak, so they were forced to switch their approach to the West branch. Forging up the West branch, the climbers followed a route that has since become popular with hundreds of New Zealand mountaineers. The Matukituki Valley is a beautiful one, its high peaks rising above slopes clothed in the softness of mountain beech forest. In the valley floor are a series of park-like open grassy flats studded with single trees.

From a rock camp at the head of the valley, the three explored Hector Col. The following day they set up camp further down valley halfway up a leading spur, now known as French Ridge, which they hoped would give access to the Bonar Glacier and thence Mt Aspiring. On 23 November 1909, they rose at 12.30 a.m. (or 1.30 according to Captain Head) and followed snow via a ramp onto the edge of the Bonar Glacier. Before them, in the soft glow of morning, they gazed on their first real view of the whole mountain. The Bonar rolled away in a saucer-shaped depression. Above it rose the vertical wall of Aspiring's South Face. On the right was the crenellated Coxcomb Ridge, while on the left lay the sharp arête of the South West Ridge, and the single 40 degree sweep of the western ice face. Here lay their route:

up very steep snow-slopes ... which required step cutting all the way. All the rocks were so plastered with icicles that it was impossible to tackle them, so that it was just a matter of step cutting, and we at last stood on the highest point of Aspiring.

With this brief comment, Alec Graham described an ascent that ranked with the best of its time. The West Face of Aspiring was not climbed again until 1965. Later mountaineers looked at the route and believed that somehow it had got more difficult since the first ascent. Such comments were perhaps designed to salve the egos of modern climbers, for Graham, Clarke and Head were fit, and Clarke and Graham both top mountaineers. It was an achievement Graham looked back on in later life with justifiable pride.

Five years after the first ascent, the mountain was again climbed, this time by a group of inexperienced enthusiasts from Dunedin, and led by the incomparable Samuel Turner. Harold Hodgkinson, Jack Murrell and George Robertson must have wondered what they had struck when they were 'invited' – at least this was the way Sam Turner described it – Turner was to accompany them as 'leader and step cutter'. Turner's account of the expedition described in his book *Conquest of the New Zealand Alps* was couched in typically Turnerian extravagant language, with frequent disparaging remarks about his companions and hyperboles regarding his own performance. They followed the route of the first ascent party on to the Bonar Glacier, and from there climbed the North West Ridge. This was the route first spotted by Alec Graham from the Waiatoto. The difficulties of the climb were greatly exaggerated by Turner who described their efforts as 'the first climb and probably the last of Mt Aspiring's east precipices'. Turner was wrong both about the topography and the difficulty of the route. It is the easiest and the most popular way to the summit, involving only 60 metres of steep rock at the bottom, before joining a broad highway sweeping to the summit.

One of the most strikingly beautiful features of Mt Aspiring is the sharp ice ridge rising out of the Bonar Glacier and soaring to

Climbing the lower section of the South West Ridge, Bonar Glacier below. (Photo: Geoff Wayatt)

On the summit of Mt Aspiring, looking down the top of the Coxcomb Ridge to the prominent pyramid of Popes Nose. (Photo: John Nankervis)

the summit. This is the South West Ridge. Many of the climbers on Aspiring in the 1920s and early 1930s commented on the ridge's beauty, but it was not climbed until 1936. In the party were Harry Stevenson, Doug Dick and David Lewis, a powerful combination of highly motivated mountaineers. Stevenson, a farmer from North Otago, was responsible for new climbs in the Aspiring region (including the first ascent of Stargazer), in the Hopkins Valley area and at Mount Cook. Dick was Stevenson's regular climbing partner of the time. Lewis was later to achieve an international reputation as a navigator and sailor of yachts in the Pacific and Southern oceans.

The South West Ridge party took two days to get themselves established at a tent camp on rocks at the toe of the ridge. From here they made a first ascent of Popes Nose, a peak at the head of the Bonar Glacier. They then turned their attention to the ridge on 12 December 1936. Good ice conditions allowed them to crampon rapidly up until near the summit. Here the ridge ends abruptly in a vertical buttress, split on the left by a steep couloir. It took quite a struggle for Stevenson to hack his way up and, after one more rope length of climbing, arrive on the broad expanse of the

top of the North West Ridge.

Although more difficult than the North West Ridge the purity of line of the South West Ridge makes it one of New Zealand's classic ice climbs. It is a 'must' for any mountaineer who wants to sample the delights of exposure, clean climbing and a thrilling summit.

In 1940 the New Zealand Alpine Club published a small supplement to its annual journal in celebration of its fiftieth jubilee. On the last page was a striking photograph entitled 'A Challenge for the Future', depicting an impressive ice-covered ridge studded with rock towers. The challenge was the Coxcomb Ridge of Mt Aspiring, and it was taken up by a succession of mountaineers in the 1940s. Numerous attempts were repulsed, either by weather, or iced rocks. The ridge consists of a lower series of rock towers, followed by a narrow ice ridge which gives way to an upper series of rock towers and the final summit cone. The rock on the ridge was not particularly sound, and because of its exposure to the weather, the towers are often heavily iced up. It was on one of these towers in 1951 that Jack Ede, who had made a number of attempts on the route, turned back after being struck on the head by a rock. In 1951 D W Peacock, N O O'Neill and M Pemberton made a near complete ascent of the ridge. They were able finally to surmount the rock towers and pushed on to the last snowslope before the summit. The weather was deteriorating rapidly though, and despite having only easy ground ahead of them, they could not see their way and decided to retreat back down the ridge.

With so much interest focused on the route, and with one attempt resulting in near success, the first complete ascent came as an anticlimax. The *New Zealand Alpine Journal* deigned only to include a short note that on 11 January 1953, the Coxcomb Ridge had been climbed by Roy Beedham and Stuart Holmes. The *NZAJ's* rival publication, the *Canterbury Mountaineer* cocked a snook at its establishment co-publication and printed a full account by Stuart Holmes. Indeed, the final climb seems to have been quite an unplanned affair. Stuart Holmes was climbing with Dave Crow from

Mt Aspiring rising dramatically above the Bonar Glacier and the glaciated face of the Kitchener Cirque. The ridge in the foreground rises to Mt Avalanche at the right. (Photo: Craig Potton)

The South Face of Mt Aspiring. (Photo: John Nankervis)

a bivouac on the Bonar Névé (they had been lucky not to be killed near the top of the South West Ridge when Crow fell 15 metres and only by chance was Holmes able to slam in a belay). During the trip they came across Roy Beedham wandering around the Bonar on his own. After a preliminary climb on Mt Avalanche, Holmes and Beedham decided to have a crack at the Coxcomb. They climbed the lower rock towers without too much difficulty, but on the snow arête the weather began to change. Windblown snow began to settle on the rocks. Holmes wrote:

After surmounting the final rock section of the ridge which required a very ticklish rock climb around an impossible gendarme, we were confronted with the final 300 feet which consisted of snow in perfect condition for a horizontal distance of about 200 yards. Progress along this final section was made by cutting the top off the ridge. Roy and I amused ourselves by trying to maintain our balance in the midst of the gale which was raging, and by looking down the thousands of feet of precipices on either side.

The rather nonchalant approach to the climb was perhaps characteristic of the climbers, Beedham in particular. His solitary ramblings on the Bonar appear to have been typical. He was killed by an avalanche on Aoraki/Mt Cook in 1958 while trying to complete an ascent of each of the 3,000 metre peaks in one summer.

With the ascent of the Coxcomb Ridge, all the ridge routes with easy access from the Matukituki Valley had been climbed. On the far side of the mountain, however, are two superb ridges overlooking the Volta and Therma glaciers. These are the North East

Ridge which separates the Volta and Therma, and the North Buttress which rises out of the Therma directly to the summit.

First to be tackled was the North East Ridge, one of the great epics in New Zealand climbing. In December 1954 Lindsay Bruce, Ian Bagley, Brian Wilkins and R E C Scott established a snowcave on the Therma Glacier after five days swagging from the Matukituki. Clearing weather on 1 January 1955 revealed the North East Ridge to be largely free of ice. The foursome found the route narrow, exposed and rotten. By mid afternoon they had reached the junction with the Coxcomb. Between the climbers and the summit however, lay the ice arête and the upper rock towers of the Coxcomb. An added problem was the obvious deterioration in the weather. By dark, they had only just started on the towers, so they retreated a short way and dug a shallow snowcave into the side of the ice arête. The night passed in some misery and the morning brought no relief. The storm raged all day, and in mid afternoon an electrical storm broke, with each climber receiving shocks. That night the wind changed to the south, a sign of clearing weather, but the accompanying fall in temperature froze their already sodden clothing and equipment. Luckily the morning was fine, but in their weakened state it took 12 hours for the four to climb the final 460 metres to the summit. In the process they were overtaken by four Auckland climbers, Jack Rattenbury, Dick Tornquist, Ivan Pickens and J D Rockell who had made a one day ascent of the North East Ridge from a camp near the site of the present Colin Todd Hut. By this time the weather was again deteriorating. While the Aucklanders scuttled down the North West Ridge to shelter, the four Otago climbers, in their battered state, were only able to make the upper rocks of the North West Ridge when a combination of darkness and driving snow forced a halt. Bruce wrote:

Lack of food or drink had now somewhat lowered our morale but we huddled together and prepared, in cheerless, chilled resignation, for the passing of the dark hours till dawn. Eventually daylight came but not the hoped for improvement in the weather. Driving snow reduced visibility to almost nil, rendering us immobile.

By two in the afternoon they had had enough and despite the weather battled their way down cutting off the North West Ridge and belaying down the steep ice ramp onto the Bonar, which they reached at 7.30 p.m. But an end to their tribulations was not quite at hand. They were forced to spend another night without food, warmth or water in an abandoned snowhole on the edge of the Bonar before reaching their camp on the Therma 'four days and one and a half hours after we had left it'. Bagley and Wilkins elected to walk out immediately, but Bruce and Scott stayed, only to find that trench foot confined them to their snowcave for five days and that when they finally came to walk out, the state of their feet slowed them so much they were forced to bivouac twice before reaching the gentler environment of the Matukituki Valley.

In contrast to the ascent of the North East Ridge, the ascent of the North Buttress the following year was a picnic. The mountain was clear of ice yet the glaciers were relatively free of bad crevassing. In February 1956, Roland Rodda teamed up with visiting American climbers Dick Irvin and Peter Robinson. Rodda was an old Aspiring campaigner and knew his way around the mountain blindfolded, while Robinson and Irvin provided a high level of technical expertise. At 10.30 a.m. on 20 January they set off from their tent camp on the Shipowner Ridge for what was intended to be a reconnaissance of the buttress. By 1 p.m. they had reached the bottom of the route. Emboldened by the clear rock and stable-looking weather they pushed on, up a series of four buttresses. The climbing was excellent and by 4.30 p.m. they were at the foot of a short ridge leading to the summit. From there, it was only a romp back to their camp. The reconnaissance had turned into a full blown climb, and their route had turned out to be a minor classic – interesting but not overly difficult climbing on an aesthetic route of good quality rock in a sunny position.

With all the mountain's ridges climbed, Aspiring had to wait another 15 years before a new way was found to the summit, via the South Face. To all climbers breasting the top of French Ridge, their first sight of Aspiring is the mountain's 500 metre south wall.

When viewed from either the South West or Coxcomb Ridge, it seems appallingly steep. Neither is there an obvious line or feature on the face, other than a band of overhangs near the bottom which guards the approach. Nevertheless, the face was climbed in 1971, but the ascent was surrounded by controversy. At 9 a.m. on Christmas Day 1971 Pete Moore and Revell Bennett appeared at the door of the French Ridge Hut, obviously weary. 'Where have you been?' asked the occupants. 'The South Face of Aspiring', was the reply. The hut occupants, and later pundits, were sceptical. Moore and Bennett's gear seemed to be dry and showed little sign of two nights bivouacking. And who were these climbers? To the status-conscious in-crowd of the early 1970s, how could these nobodies have climbed the South Face? Nevertheless, Moore and Bennett almost certainly did make the climb, and in difficult circumstances. From a bivouac in a crevasse at the foot of the face, they left at 12 noon on a reconnaissance up an ice ramp on the left side of the face. Rapid progress lifted their hopes and they headed right on steepening ice. As the terrain became more difficult, Moore and Bennett noticed to their concern, that retreat was not going to be easy: night was coming on and the weather was deteriorating. They had encountered a classical mountaineering trap – climbing to a position where the difficulties of retreat seemed to offer more dangers than pressing on, even over unknown ground. Moore wrote:

We traversed diagonally across mixed snow and ice slopes (55–70°), keeping one torch in use most of the time. By now we were only vaguely sure of where our route would lead us … Another two hours of painfully slow progress brought us to the summit ridge with snow flakes whipping at our faces. I pulled out my North Wall hammer by its wrist sling only to see it fall out of sight into the waiting empty blackness. I couldn't have cared less about this development.

It was 2 a.m., it was snowing, and their torch batteries were flat. But in Moore's words, 'we pushed our luck once more' and descended the South West Ridge to regain the bivouac at 5 a.m.

It was a truly remarkable performance, and in view of the night-time, torchless descent, it seemed hardly surprising that many conservative climbers questioned their climb. But the doubters took a knock four months later when in May 1972 the face received a second ascent, this time by Bill Denz and Limbo Thompson, who, although following a slightly different line, confirmed Moore's route description. And to put paid to all questioning Pete Moore and Revell Bennett returned to the face, in winter and by helicopter access. Climbing on a special 180 metre rope, Moore led the whole climb. Bennett, who had lost fingers in an industrial accident the previous year, belayed and followed Moore on jumars for five pitches. Then he stopped. Moore headed on alone on self belay up to a 65° gully direct to the summit. He then rappelled back to Bennett and back down the face to a waiting helicopter. Five hours to the summit, one and a half hours down, and 15 minutes out!

In January 1978 Don Bogie and Ken Hyslop explored the North Face of Aspiring, a section of the mountain lying between the North East Ridge and North Buttress. The face is quite short, no more than 480 metres. The bottom two-thirds is steep, sound rock. The upper section lies back and is either snow-covered, or comprises loose rock terraces. Bogie and Hyslop found to their satisfaction that there was a prominent rib in the centre of the face. The rock proved excellent, with a sunny location and enjoyable climbing. The upper section was not quite so outstanding however. The route lay under the ice-encrusted rocks of the upper Coxcomb Ridge, and the afternoon sun loosened frequent fusillades of ice particles on the climbers as they hurried to the safety of the summit ridge. Having been warned of the dangers, Mark Edgar and Brian Weedon chose March 1981 to create another route on the North Face, left of the Bogie/Hyslop route. At that time of year the upper slopes were free of ice, and the lower sections of eight rope lengths all on good rock. This part of the face now provides a challenge for rock climbers, and new variations are appearing year after year.

When Don Bogie and Ken Hyslop climbed the North Face of Aspiring, that left only one unclimbed flank on the mountain, the North East Face. The *Mt Aspiring Guidebook* read:

The North East Ridge on the left, North East Face and North Buttress (centre), North Face and North West Ridge of Mt Aspiring at the far right. (Photo: Craig Potton)

The unclimbed northeast face lies between the northeast and Coxcomb ridges, and would require a bivvy on the Volta Névé. The face presents an enormous expanse of rather featureless rock nearly 600 metres high. A snow lead present at least until early February might provide a route up the lower half.

The route description was to predict almost precisely the way the face was finally climbed. But the nature of the ascent was audacious. The Volta Glacier is one of the most remote in New Zealand, and retreat in the event of accident or storm almost impossi-

ble. So when Bogie and Lindsay Bell crossed the ridge bordering the Bonar Glacier in August 1979, and began rappelling to a bivouac site on the Volta, they knew they were burning their bridges. They were committed to succeeding – or else.

The weather was not perfect: an icy wind blew, and storm clouds hovered to the west. Once onto the face, the pair were troubled by falling ice blocks. Bogie wrote:

none [were] bigger than a fist, but even so they are more than just annoying. If you are climbing when you hear a lot coming you just

Mt Aspiring reflected in a tarn on Cascade Saddle, looking across the Matukituki Valley.
(Photo: Colin Monteath/Hedgehog House)

plant both axes and wait till they whine and buzz past. If you are belaying you tighten your grip on the rope and wait. On country like this you can't move anywhere in a hurry.

After only 150 metres Bogie and Bell found they had climbed onto tricky ground with iced-up loose rock below one band of overhangs and above another. They knew their only chance of success lay in traversing right to gain the prominent gully. To do this they were forced into nerve-wracking climbing. Their belay anchors were poor, and the ice too thin to ensure sound ice screw protection. Feeling relief, they pulled round into the gully, and the relative security of solid snow and ice. Now it was a matter of just grinding the route down until they reached the top. Dusk found the climb-ers breasting the Coxcomb Ridge, but still with a good 300 metres in height and half a kilometre to the summit. They elected to bivouac. The morning brought deteriorating weather. Knowing the difficulties of the upper Coxcomb Ridge even in summer, let alone in August, Bogie reluctantly chose to traverse the slopes at the top of the North Face route he had climbed with Ken Hyslop seven months previously. The wind grew in strength, bowing the rope linking him to Bell in a huge arc. By late afternoon, as they struggled onto the summit, it was shrieking round the mountain. 'We spent about thirty seconds stuffing my rope in my pack' and headed off down the North West Ridge towards the safety and calm of the Matukituki Valley.

NORTH WEST RIDGE

SOUTH WEST RIDGE

THE BUTTRESS

RAMP

BONAR NÉVÉ

Photo: Craig Potton

MT ASPIRING
Classic Route: South West Ridge

Access: Walk up the Matukituki Valley via Shovel Flat to Pearl Flat and ascend a steep bush track to French Ridge. Tussock slopes on French Ridge lead to the Lucas-Trotter Hut. It is a day's walk to the hut.

The Climb: From Lucas-Trotter Hut walk up the ridge above the hut and, when under Mt French, follow right up the ice slope of the Quarterdeck, to reach the Bonar Glacier névé. Cross the névé and climb close under the South Face onto the lower South West Ridge. From here the ridge is a narrow snow arête leading 300 metres up to a vertical rock step about 50 metres below the summit. Climb the rock step via a gully on the left. The summit is near at hand.

Descend via the North West Ridge, an easy route especially if followed all the way to the gap in the Shipowner Ridge. It is a long trudge back via the Bonar Glacier to the Quarterdeck and French Ridge. Closer shelter is available at the Colin Todd on the Shipowner Ridge below the North West Ridge. There is an alternative snow and ice route off the North West Ridge on the west side. Called 'The Ramp', it is a quick descent route for competent climbers, but there have been many fatalities.

First Ascent: Harry Stevenson, Doug Dick, David Lewis: 12 December 1936

Grade 3-

Mt Tapuae-o-Uenuku from the north, with the upper Hodder Valley in the foreground. Staircase Creek (centre), the summit of Tapuae-o-Uenuku (left) and Mt Alarm to the right. (Photo: Craig Potton)

MT TAPUAE-O-UENUKU

Mt Tapuae-o-Uenuku is one of New Zealand's great landmarks. It can be seen from over 100 kilometres to the north, seeming to shimmer above the blue waters of Cook Strait.

The mountain has influenced the people living around it from earliest times. Archaeological records indicate that the northeast coast of the South Island was the location of very early Polynesian settlement, around 900 AD. Tapuae-o-Uenuku is prominent when viewed from important moa hunter sites at the Wairau Bar and the Clarence River mouth. The Clarence (Waiau-Toa) River site was occupied over the centuries by the early hunter-gatherers and by Ngatimamoe and Ngai Tahu tribes. Tapuae-o-Uenuku's summit is only 24 kilometres from the river mouth, and in a space of eight kilometres rises 2,500 metres. It is no wonder then that the mountain features in tribal myths and legends and that its name, meaning Footsteps of the Rainbow God, is an ancient and revered one.

Tapuae-o-Uenuku is the highest point of the Inland Kaikoura range. The range, like all of New Zealand's mountains (except the volcanoes) has been pushed up as the Australian and Pacific tectonic plates collide, compress and thrust under each other. The Kaikoura mountains are very young geologically and are the result of very rapid mountain uplift, dating back perhaps no more than 500,000 years. They are being pushed up probably at seven or more millimetres per year as a block between two parts of the great Alpine Fault that marks the boundary between the Indo–Australian and Pacific plates. Further south this fault forms the spectacular steep scarp of the Southern Alps as they rise abruptly from the narrow South Westland coastal plain. Here, the mountains just east of the Alpine Fault are being raised at extremely rapid rates of more than 10 millimetres a year. However, erosion, driven by the 10 metres of rain that falls each year, balances this rapid uplift and the mountains grow no higher. The Kaikouras are different for it seems that their very rapid uplift is not balanced by rapid erosion – the climate is too dry. Thus it would seem that the Kaikouras grow a bit taller each year.

The Kaikoura mountains are slightly different geologically from the rest of the Southern Alps. While containing the same greywacke sediments that make up the Alps, these sediments have been intruded by a large body of volcanic rock, which explains the red rocks found high on Tapuae-o-Uenuku. At the foot of the range where uplift has been less, younger rocks including limestone are found (limestone outcrops are particularly noticeable in the Chalk Range immediately east of Tapuae-o-Uenuku).

Tapuae-o-Uenuku is situated in one of the hottest, driest regions of New Zealand. Temperatures regularly exceed 30°C in summer, but correspondingly can plunge in winter to below –20°C. Snow can be found in small pockets near the summit even in the middle of summer. There are no glaciers, although there are some of the best and probably most active rock glaciers in New Zealand

The two Hodder Huts, Hodder Valley. (Photo: David Chowdhury)

Descending a scree track near the Hodder Huts. (Photo: David Chowdhury)

under Tapuae-o-Uenuku and Alarm. These are large deposits of rock scree with frozen cores, which cause them to flow like ice glaciers. The countryside around Tapuae-o-Uenuku was forested originally but these forests were probably destroyed in fires early in the Polynesian era about 700 years ago. Today, after further burning by pastoralists, patches of mountain totara and lacebark are found only in isolated gullies. Elsewhere the lower slopes carry manuka scrub and khaki-brown tussocks and grasses. The upper slopes are windswept scree and rock shattered by freezing and thawing.

Mountaineering and Tapuae-o-Uenuku have a chequered beginning, linked with a feud between Governor George Grey and his deputy, Lieutenant Governor Edward Eyre. In November 1849 Eyre climbed from the Awatere Valley up the Hodder River to 'about 300 yards in distance and about 50 feet in elevation of the very highest point' of Tapuae-o-Uenuku in order to survey access routes between Marlborough and Canterbury. Eyre had made the climb against the advice of Grey's secretary, William Hamilton, who was in Eyre's party. In addition, the descent (which was made at night)

was marred by tragedy. Wiremu Hoeta of Wellington slipped on ice and was killed. Eyre too only narrowly missed falling off.

The incident provided Grey with an excuse for accusing his Lieutenant Governor of incompetence. Grey and Eyre were both strong-minded and egotistical. Both fancied themselves as explorers. Eyre in fact had made a name for himself by an epic 2,000 kilometre trek round the coast of the Great Australian Bight. Grey was the more able politician, however, and eventually engineered Eyre's removal.

The first recorded complete ascent of Tapuae-o-Uenuku was made by Nehemiah McRae, probably in 1864, from the Gladstone Station in the Awatere Valley and via the Hodder River. McRae left a bottle and a note recording his ascent, and reputedly a five pound note. Herein lies a story. The five pound note apparently disappeared after the next ascent in 1874 but was replaced in 1876 by a cheque for £1,000,000. In 1882, when the mountain was climbed from the eastern Clarence River side by F Trolove, A Brown, G S McRae, and two women, Mrs Gale and Mrs Stephenson Smith, the cheque was still there but, unfortunately, it was unsigned!

Since then Tapuae-o-Uenuku has been climbed by various routes. These include Tongue Spur which separates the Hodder and Shin rivers, and routes from the Shin River via the Bridge Spur and Crows Nest. From the upper Hodder there are direct routes up via Staircase Creek, and over Pinnacle. From the east, the routes from the Clarence Valley via the Dee and Branch streams are, in the words of noted botanist John Scott-Thomson 'interesting botanically but can have no great appeal to the climber'. He wasn't right on this last remark. The ascent of the mountain from the east is definitely more scenic than from the west. Its only drawback is the requirement for four wheel drive access over a private road to the Branch cottage. From here, an open tussock and scree ridge gives access to the beautiful upper Branch Creek. Plentiful camping sites allow climbers access to the Tapuae-o-Uenuku – Alarm col, or the upper northern slopes beside Pinnacle, or to the unclimbed South Face.

Tapuae-o-Uenuku from the west after an autumn snowfall. (Photo: John Nankervis)

Winter, however, presents a greater challenge. More than a few parties have returned from the mountain down the Hodder River, with its 80 or so river crossings, suffering frostbite. The first winter ascent was made this way in August 1922 by Frank Milne and G H Seddon. In June 1946 Ed Hillary, W F Hillary and A Robb traversed from the Hodder to the Dee, collecting some frostbite on the way.

While Tapuae-o-Uenuku may not present great obstacles to the mountaineer, it provides nevertheless a good outdoor experience. The approach up a valley like the Hodder cannot be taken lightly, as its endless river crossings and swift mountain current can trap the unwary. The climb up the mountain is usually straightforward. Yet it gives superb views of the inland plains of Marlborough and the rugged coastline north of Kaikoura. To know Tapuae-o-Uenuku is to know one of New Zealand's great mountains.

Cramponning in winter conditions up to the summit of Tapuae-o-Uenuku. (Photo: David Chowdhury)

TAPUAE-O-UENUKU

ALARM

STAIRCASE CREEK

THE BUTTRESS

(Photo: Craig Potton)

MT TAPUAE-O-UENUKU
Classic Route: Hodder Valley, South Ridge

Access: As the access and the climb form a single expedition, they are described together. A round tip from the road normally takes three days.

Starting from the Awatere Valley road at Gladstone Station, it is six to seven hours walk up the Hodder River. In its upper sections the Hodder flows through a narrow gorge. Many river crossings are necessary. A track bypasses a waterfall on the true right bank. Above the waterfall, tussock terraces lead to the Hodder Hut. Above the hut walk up-valley and then follow Staircase Creek into the basins under Mt Alarm. Climb easy slopes towards the saddle between Tapuae-o-Uenuku and

Mt Alarm, angling left under a small rocky peak onto the flat section well above the saddle, and then up the South Ridge to the summit.

The descent can be made the same way, or alternatively, follow the North Ridge towards Pinnacle, dropping down a gully just before Pinnacle.

First Ascent: Nehemiah McRae: 1864.

Grade 3

D'Archiac's South Face (at left) and South East Ridge (right) rise up above Separation Col. (Photo: Mark Sedon/Off Piste Photography)

MT D'ARCHIAC

D'Archiac stood guard, a towering mass of fluted ice and snow over the lesser peaks of the Godley.

On a clear day from near the coast of the mid Canterbury Plains and viewed west across the farmland and brown tussock foothills, a great pyramidal peak of snow and ice stands out from the ranges of the Southern Alps. This peak is D'Archiac, the patriarch of the Rangitata and Godley watershed. It is a mountain which inevitably draws the mountaineer, both as an object of beauty and as a challenge.

D'Archiac is the anchor point of the northern boundary of Aoraki/Mount Cook National Park, and the highest summit for over 300 kilometres between the Mount Cook peaks and Mt Tapuae-o-Uenuku. On the mountain's south side the Godley Glacier curls away 10 kilometres to the southeast. To the north, the incised Forbes Valley carves down to the Havelock branch of the Rangitata River. The mountain has four major ridges: the West Ridge splits and forms the northwest and southwest outliers above the Godley Glacier terminal; the North Ridge runs down beside the Dennistoun Glacier and drops into the main ice stream of the Godley; to the east, the icy East Ridge and the rock buttresses of the South East Ridge both rise from high cols between the Forbes Glacier and the Godley watershed. From all directions, D'Archiac is a mountain of stature and dominance. In the words of Jim Dennistoun, who made the first ascent, it is 'a splendid fellow but a big nut to crack'.

Dennistoun climbed the mountain on 12 March 1910 with guide Jack Clarke and Lawrence Earle. They climbed from the Forbes Valley, under the impression that they were scaling a nearby peak, Mt McClure. Only on reaching a high col which they appropriately named Revelation Col, did they realise that the giant above them was D'Archiac. Dennistoun, who had earlier explored much of the headwaters of the Rangitata Valley, was eager to press on, even though it was late in the day and they still had the steep East Ridge in front of them. From his home at Mt Peel, Dennistoun had a fine view of D'Archiac and badly wanted to climb the mountain. His enthusiasm won over Clarke and a very reluctant Earle. They pressed on up the East Ridge and made the summit late in the day. Their penalty was benightment on rock slopes above the North Forbes Glacier.

Other routes were not climbed for another 20 years. Neville Johnston, H J Newberry and Ian Powell climbed the North Ridge on a misty day in December 1934, revelling in the sound rock on the upper portions of the ridge. The West Ridge was climbed from the small Trident Glacier in 1935 by W H Scott, P F Scully, A Thompson and Betty Lorimer, but its southwest outlier had to wait until 1977 when climbed by Brian Turner and Philip Temple, while the northwest outlier is unclimbed. The North Face snow slope was skied by Mark Sedon and Kane Henderson in 1999.

The most difficult ridge route on D'Archiac is probably the

Kane Henderson on the summit of D'Archiac, about to make the first ski descent. (Photo: Mark Sedon/Off Piste Photography)

The Forbes Valley and the eastern side of D'Archiac, with Mistake Flat hut at the bush edge (centre). (Photo: Shaun Barnett/Black Robin Photography)

South East Ridge. This ridge rises from Separation Col, between the Forbes Valley and the Separation tributary of the Godley. It was climbed in February 1951 by Stan Conway, Bernie McClelland, Jack Pattle, Trevor James and John Sampson from a tent camp on the South Forbes Glacier névé. Their climb up the rock and ice ridge was slow but by 6 p.m. they had surmounted the ridge's three steps and made the summit. The climbers descended as night fell and were forced to bivouac halfway down the East Ridge. The night was like so many bivouacs high in the mountains. Time passed slowly, and the climbers, lacking sleeping bags, intermittently shivered and dozed, watching as the hard cold starlight too slowly gave way to the pale light of dawn and the long awaited warming rays of sunrise.

The South East Ridge also has had a winter ascent. Isolation, a heavy coating of snow and ice, and the exposed position makes the ridge a serious winter climb. Rob Rainsbury and Eric Saggers, who made the ascent in July 1979, found the route challenging. Saggers reported:

… ice runnels, and now and again snow built up on the ridge into a sharp arête. We sat astride one of these arêtes as though we were on the back of a horse. On the last step Rob scraped about on some awkward ice; he needed to be six feet further to his right but a slight bulge in the terrain caused some anxious moments for both of us as I had an almost useless belay directly below him.

Rainsbury made the moves however, and he and Saggers completed the climb.

D'Archiac's classic climbs lie on its ridges at present. There are routes on its faces, though. The northern flank in particular, is a popular and rapid route to the summit from the Dennistoun Glacier via moderately angled snow slopes. The unclimbed South Face was a more serious proposition, in that it is nearly 900 metres high. It was climbed by Bill McLeod and Peter Dickson in November 1992 via a prominent snow gully just right of a central rock buttress and above up a rib to the summit ridge. Legend has it McLeod's crampon was broken, hence the route was named 'The Band-Aid Route' to commemorate the elastoplast holding the crampon together.

Mountaineering is one aspect of D'Archiac but the peak is also intimately linked with the history of the surrounding countryside. The Ngai Tahu Maori called D'Archiac, or at least the region around it, Kahui Kaupeka, the assembly of riverheads. Ngai Tahu from Waimate and Arowhenua spent each summer on the plains of the MacKenzie Country catching birds for winter storage. Some parties ranged up the Godley, at least as far as the terminal of the Godley Glacier. There is some debate about whether Sealy Pass, at the head of the Godley Glacier, was an occasional access route to West Coast greenstone country. The heavier glaciation of the seventeenth and eighteenth century may have made the Godley a serious proposition to ascend, with more icefalls and crevasses, but the higher levels of the glacier may also have made it easier to cross Sealy Pass, which now has a steep ice slope on the Godley side. Similarly, Maori may also have crossed Gunn Pass at the head of the Havelock branch of the Rangitata, but again, the record is unclear, just as the explorations of many nineteenth century goldminers (who did ascend Gunn Pass) are often unknown.

Mt D'Archiac with the South West Ridge (centre), South Face, South East Ridge (right)
and Separation Col. (Photo: Don Bogie)

In the 1850s and 1860s the tussock downs of the Godley and Rangitata valleys were invaded by pastoralists seeking sheep grazing. By 1857 all the Canterbury foothills were taken up by the immigrants of the Canterbury Association so that latecomers were forced to explore further inland for their grazing. In 1855 pioneer pastoralists Charles Tripp and J B A Acland went up the Havelock as far as the Forbes River, before settling further down valley at Peel Forest and Orari. In 1860 Samuel Butler and John Baker similarly went to the head of the Havelock, but found no suitable grazing. Butler stayed on however, at Mesopotamia Station on the south bank of the Rangitata. It was here that Julius von Haast stayed during the Rangitata stage of his survey of the Canterbury Province. And it was Haast who was to name D'Archiac, along with a host of other features.

Over a period of five years Haast surveyed almost all the alpine valleys between Arthur's and Haast Pass. In 1861 he was in the Rangitata, and in 1862 the Godley. After staying with Butler, Haast and his companion Sinclair journeyed up the Havelock, naming the river after Sir Henry Havelock, a British commander during the Indian Mutiny. Haast also went up the North Forbes (which he named after James Forbes, a British glaciologist) as far as the glacier. The following year Haast was up the Godley – naming the glacier after John Robert Godley, one of the founders of the Canterbury settlement. Unlike the Rangitata, Haast was not preceded up the Godley by graziers, and so was probably the first European onto the glacier. During each of these explorations Haast noted the 'colossal pyramid!' as he called the mountain 'rising in stern solemnity above the vast snowfields'. The only problem he had was in naming the mountain. Haast's initial reports refer variously to a Mt Tyndall, and a Mt Forbes. It was only a couple of years later that he settled on the name of D'Archiac. As with so many of Haast's place names, the Vicomte D'Archiac was a man of science, a Director of the Museum of Geology in Paris, and as at least some have noted, a man who could have assisted Haast's scientific career amongst the establishment in Europe. D'Archiac committed suicide however, in 1868, driven either from losses on the stock exchange or, some speculated, from a number of different wives.

It seems strange that D'Archiac should carry the name of someone with little association with either the mountain or the surrounding land, but such are the vagaries of nomenclature. The name does have a noble sound to it however. And appropriately so for a mountain which is lord of the surrounding country.

Above: Approaching the summit of D'Archiac. (Photo: John Nankervis)
Left: Looking across from Sealy Pass to the western side of D'Archiac.
(Photo: Geoff Spearpoint)

Photo: Institute of Geological & Nuclear Sciences

MT D'ARCHIAC
Classic Route: East Ridge

Access: The ridge is usually approached from the Havelock. Using a four-wheel drive vehicle to Finday Bush Hut helps save time.

From Erewhon sheep station, cross the Clyde River (difficult in high water) and then follow the north bank of the Havelock River. At Freezing Point, cross the Havelock and head straight up-valley to the Forbes River. The Forbes is easy going all the way to the South Forbes Glacier. It is about six hours walk to here from Erewhon. There is a small hut in the South Forbes, but it is often better to bivouac further up valley.

To reach the foot of the ridge, climb rock bluffs on the south side of the South Forbes icefall, and then wind up through crevasses to Revelation Col.

The Climb: Above Revelation Col climb easy rock and snow, until reaching a final rock buttress. At this point move left into a snow gully and climb up this for about 200 metres to the summit ridge. From here follow the corniced, or in late summer, blocky ridge to the top.

Descend the same way.

First Ascent: Jack Clarke, Jim Dennistoun, Lawrence Earle: 12 March 1910.

Grade 2

MT EARNSLAW

Mt Earnslaw is the largest peak in the complex area of mountains and valleys at the head of Lake Wakatipu. Thousands of years ago, the huge glaciers that carved the serpentine shape of Wakatipu were split at their head either side of the Earnslaw massif. As the glaciers receded, leaving the lake behind them, they created the twin valleys of the Dart and the Rees. With the warming climate, beech forests reinvaded the valleys and crept up the slopes of the Forbes Mountains, the group of peaks which Earnslaw dominates. Above the forest level however, the glaciers remain, and at 2,835 metres, Earnslaw is high enough to still be glaciated. The mountain is more bulky than graceful. It consists of two summits connected by a one and a half kilometre long ridge. The East and West peaks in turn each have southern ridges leading off towards the lower Dart and Rees valleys, and northern ridges towards the Main Divide ranges. On the eastern side, the peak has two large glaciers feeding the Lennox Creek and the Earnslaw Burn. On the north bare rocky slopes lead down into the Bedford Stream.

Earnslaw is not a challenging peak to the mountaineer in the way that Aoraki/Mt Cook or Mt Tutoko are. Framed in the waters of Lake Wakatipu, it is however a beautiful mountain which catches the attention of those who visit the lake.

Both the lake and mountain have been a focus for much human activity over the centuries. To Maori the area was important, first as a hunting ground for food such as the moa, and later as a source of the prized greenstone for implements, ornaments and weapons. Carbon dates for Maori sites in the area date back to at least 1300 AD. Their name for Mt Earnslaw was Pikirakatahi. Harsh winter weather however, meant Maori usually visited here in the summer only. It was not until the arrival of Europeans in the 1850s that larger numbers of people began to settle more permanently around the mountain.

The first Europeans to arrive at Wakatipu were those who sought to live off the land. W G Rees took up a sheep run at Queenstown in 1860 and stocked land at the head of the lake in 1861. Soon after the sheep farmers came those who sought their living in the ground, the gold prospectors. Between 1861 and 1863 the surveyor James McKerrow reported groups of prospectors well up the Rees River, and by 1863 gold seekers had penetrated beyond Earnslaw, and crossed the Main Divide ranges. In 1864 prospector A J Barrington began his epic ventures into the Olivine Ice Plateau to the west. Also at this time surveyor John Turnbull Thomson named the mountain after his father's village in Scotland. Earnslaw is an old English word, meaning Eagle's Hill, an appropriate term for the peak.

The economic exploitation of the Earnslaw area was followed by recreational exploitation. The famous scenery of Lake Wakatipu attracted tourists. Accommodation houses sprang up at Queenstown in the 1860s and in the late 1870s at Glenorchy at the head of the lake. To some who came for their holidays, the surrounding moun-

Left: The steep and dramatic eastern faces of the West and East Peak of Earnslaw rise from the head of the Earnslaw Burn. (Photo: Craig Potton)
Above: West Peak (left) and East Peak (right) of Mt Earnslaw. (Photo: Craig Potton)

The new and old Esquilant Bivvies on Wright Col. The East Peak of Earnslaw, and easiest ascent route crosses the upper scree terrace and up the upper rock bluffs directly above the hut. (Photo: Wayne Marshall/Hedgehog House)

tains provided a means of exercise. Indeed, the earliest recorded recreational mountaineering in New Zealand occurred here, such as Francis Huddleston's ascent of Cleft Peak at the head of the Rees Valley in 1874. In March 1882 the Rev W S Green, Emil Boss and Ulrich Kaufmann, finding a week on their hands after their attempt on Aoraki/Mt Cook, and before their boat sailed for Europe, dashed to the head of Lake Wakatipu to attempt Mt Earnslaw. Steaming up the lake by small paddle boat, Green described the view:

The white glaciers of Mt Earnslaw shone through the mists, now and then we could distinguish one of the twin peaks of its summit, and bright gleams of sunshine danced on the surface of the lake, giving glorious effects of sunlight and shadow, and filling us with the brightest hopes.

Their hopes were dashed though, well short of the summit, by heavy rain and snow.

One of those who helped Green's party was the son of the proprietor of the Mt Earnslaw hotel at Glenorchy. This was Harry Birley, a man with both an adventurous spirit and entrepreneurial streak. Earnslaw was on his back doorstep and its lower slopes provided a suitable objective for guided parties of hotel guests. During these trips Birley explored the approaches to the peak and by 1890 knew his best chance of success lay from the east via the forest above the Lennox Creek and into a large tussock bowl named the Kea Basin. In mid-March Birley set out with Frank Muir, a photographer from Dunedin. Within two days they had climbed to a high col on the range. From there Birley pushed on alone and hewed a line of steps up 300 metres of ice on the East Face, to reach the summit of the East Peak on 16 March 1890. He left a flagged rock cairn containing a shilling.

Birley's approach to the mountain via the Rees Valley, and up to Kea Basin and the Birley Glacier proved a popular one. In 1892 the East Peak was ascended again, by Malcolm and Kenneth Ross, up an easier route via bluffs and scree slopes on the northeast flank. This route has now become the most popular way to climb Mt Earnslaw. The Ross's were accompanied most of the way by Mrs Ross, D McConnochy and Birley. Indeed, Birley began to ply his trade on Earnslaw, guiding it at least three more times.

For many years the West Peak of Earnslaw was regarded as higher than the East Peak. In fact it is approximately 14 metres lower. From most directions the West Peak is more magnificent than its eastern neighbour. While the East Peak is rounded and softened by snow slopes and glaciers, the West Peak is craggier and more turret-shaped. One feature is particularly prominent. From the head of the Bedford Stream, the West Peak stands up like a great fluted pillar, with the rocks of the North Face forming a striking buttress. This feature attracted the attention of Frank Wright, one of the most talented mountaineers in New Zealand in the early twentieth century. In February 1914 Wright, accompanied by John Robertson, started from the Earnslaw Hut below the Kea Basin. They ascended the Birley Glacier, crossed the col (later to be named Wright Col), between the East Peak and Mt Leary, and traversed

Descending off the higher East Peak, with the West Peak of Earnslaw behind. (Photo: Nick Groves)

steep snow slopes across the head of the valley. Wright had noted a spectacular gully up the rocks of the North Face which he hoped would lead to the unclimbed summit. The route measured up to Wright's expectations. For 450 metres the rock climbed by the pair yielded some most interesting situations, a euphemistic description for steep climbing. The final stretch lay up a snow pyramid considerably steeper than the roof of a house. At 4.30 p.m., 12 hours after leaving camp they reached the summit.

With both the East and West peaks having been climbed, mountaineers turned to newer approaches to the mountain. It was some time after Wright and Robertson's 1914 efforts, however, before the spirit of adventure drove climbers to new ground. In the early 1930s a band of enthusiastic Dunedin climbers flocked to the Rees and Dart valleys. First to the fray were Jock Sim, Andy Jackson, John Knowles and Scott Gilkison. In 1932 they climbed from the

Spaniard Valley up to Pluto Col and onto the North West Ridge of the West Peak. Pleasant, and unexpectedly firm rock led them upwards. One particularly steep section forced the quartet onto the northern flank, but it was soon overcome and they reached the summit. Their route is the most enjoyable way to get to the West Peak, but shouldn't be underestimated.

Flushed with success, Jackson and Gilkison ascended the East Peak two days later, via a new route up the glaciated East Flank. With two first ascents to their credit, Jackson and Gilkison returned for a third on 11 January! They climbed the standard North Flank route on the East Peak and then cramponned down the arête linking the West Peak. The section rising up to the West Peak provided steep, very exposed rock and ice climbing. This Grand Traverse, while not matching up quite to the spectacular nature of the better-known Grand Traverse of Mt Cook, was nonetheless a superb

From Wright Col looking across to the West Peak with the North Ridge in profile and Mt Pluto on the right. (Photo: Colin Monteath/Hedgehog House)

climb, moving a later climber, Colin Todd, to write:

> *... it is the finest climb available from the Esquilant Bivouac. Yes! It would go, but mighty steep. What an exhilarating slope! However did the Earnslaw Glacier hang there?*

Thus in the space of two weeks, three first ascents had been snatched, with two of them, the North West Ridge and the traverse, being plums. When linked together as an ascent of the North West Ridge of the West Peak and traverse to the East Peak, they form one of New Zealand's classic alpine climbs.

There remained in the 1930s one more significant new route. In March 1935, Vern Leader set off from the Earnslaw Hut and crossed Wright Col. The season had been fine and the mountain largely clear of snow. Across the head of Bedford Stream were only scree slopes rather than the usual steep snow. Leader tripped quickly across the scree and then, beneath the lowest part of the East–West Peak ridge, climbed onto the ridge. But where Jackson and Gilkison had been able to climb on the east on good snow, Leader found hard, bare ice. Rather than tackle such conditions alone, Leader took to the rocks on the west and climbed up two steep rock ribs to the summit of the West Peak.

Earnslaw, particularly the East Peak, continued to be a popular climb throughout the thirties and after the Second World War. The mountain was comparatively accessible, and the East Peak via the North Flank offered a relatively easy ascent of a spectacular-looking mountain. There was however, still some novelty left. In a period of one year, 1953, three more new routes were climbed. The first was the mountain's last unclimbed ridge. This was the Seven Sisters Ridge, a rather jumbled affair leading from the South West Ridge up onto the West Peak. The route had repulsed a number of parties, and had a reputation for loose rock.

In February 1953, however, a close examination of the route by D W Beatty, Jim McNulty, M M McNaught and P A L Fraser, showed the ridge was more of a paper tiger than was thought. The large blocks on the ridge proved to be avoidable by traversing. The next climb was a new route on the East Face of the East Peak via a line further west than that taken in 1933. Roland Rodda, Murray Ellis and O L Wynn ascended a long, wide, icy 40° couloir leading up to the shoulder high on the southern ridge of the East Peak. During the climb, Rodda eyed up a new approach to the West Peak further across the head of the Earnslaw Glacier. Rodda returned in February 1953 with Fred Hollows, crossed further across the same shelf he used to gain access to this East Peak route, and climbed slopes on the edge of the East Face of the West Peak to gain the upper sections of the ridge connecting the East and West Peaks.

Since the 1953 ascents, Earnslaw has been the focus of new climbs on only two occasions. In January 1973 Pete Glasson and Colin Strang climbed direct up the bluffs in the Earnslaw Burn. There they chose a hard ice rib leading up the East Face of the West Peak, guarded on either side by ice cliffs, but aesthetic and free of objective danger for 25 or more rope lengths. Nine years later the face was climbed again, this time in winter by a route further left. Kim Logan and Mike Roberts reported 'a great deal of water ice was encountered and following a bivvy at 1,700 metres, above Gilkinson Stream, we reached the summit at 2 a.m. on the third day. Hard ice and powder snow. Very cold'.

EAST PEAK
WEST PEAK
NORTH WEST RIDGE
WRIGHT COL

Photo: Nick Groves/Hedgehog House

MT EARNSLAW

Classic Route: North West Ridge/West Peak – East Peak Traverse

Access: From Glenorchy walk up the Rees Valley and ascend the forest track to Kea Basin. Climb up through the basins to the Esquilant Bivouac hut on Wright Col.

The Climb: From Wright Col traverse across the scree shelf above the head of Bedford Stream, angling up towards the foot of the North Ridge. Start the ridge straight up, but if any difficulties turn on the left side. Higher up the ridge narrows and flattens out just before the West Peak summit.

Begin the traverse to the East Peak by keeping on the south side. This involves steep very exposed climbing down a snow face and two steep rock steps on the east side. The climb to the East Peak is straightforward. From the East Peak descend easy slopes back towards Wright Col, descending the bluffs halfway down the face via a rock gully/wall on the western side.

First Ascent (North West Ridge): Jock Sim, Andy Jackson, John Knowles and Scott Gilkison: December 1931

Grade 3-

Mt Arrowsmith from near Couloir Peak showing the East Ridge on the left, Cameron Glacier Face (centre) and North Ridge on right. (Photo: Bill King)

MT ARROWSMITH

The stark rock battlements of Mt Arrowsmith are a feature of the country between the Rakaia and Rangitata rivers. Unlike most of the big peaks of the Southern Alps, Mt Arrowsmith lies some twenty kilometres east of the Main Divide, and hence, although just under 3,000 metres high, is in a rainshadow and consequently lacks the big snow and ice faces of the neighbouring peaks to the west. Arrowsmith is a bulky mountain, not so much striking for any beauty of line but rather as a dominating mass, with three long ridges radiating out east, southwest and north. It cradles two glaciers – the Ashburton to the south, and the Cameron on its northern side. Its approaches are up the tussock and scrub valleys of the Lawrence, Ashburton and Cameron, three typical Canterbury rivers, denuded of ancient totara forests by pre-European fires, and now characterised by grasslands, sparse high alpine vegetation, bald shingle summits and large scree slopes on the surrounding hills.

Mt Arrowsmith is one of the more accessible of New Zealand's high mountains. It is only two hours drive from Christchurch to the entrance of the mini-gorge of the lower Cameron Valley. From here an easy four hour walk, either up the Cameron Valley or over a low pass into the upper Ashburton Valley, leads to base huts from which to climb the mountain. The Lawrence Valley approach takes the same driving time but has a six hour walk.

The relatively easy access to the mountain is not reflected in the mountain's climbing history however. Samuel Butler and John Baker ascended Butler Saddle in their search for sheep country in 1860–61, in the process gaining a good view through Whitcombe Pass to the mysterious-looking forests of the West Coast – Butler's Erewhon. Von Haast, who visited the upper Ashburton in 1861, found the glacier to be:

exceedingly beautiful, the ice is quite pure and is broken half a mile above its terminal with numerous seracs, forming one of the most splendid ice cascades I ever saw.

Alas, time has taken its toll on this beauty and the glacier has receded considerably. In 1861 von Haast was up the Cameron, naming the glacier the Hawker, after his companion J Hawker, a South Australian politician. For once Haast's name did not stick and it later reverted to the Cameron Glacier.

These early explorations took place at the same time as sheep farmers moved into the Canterbury mountains. Large pastoral runs were taken up at Mt Potts and Upper Lake Heron in 1857, Lower Lake Heron (now known as Mt Arrowsmith Station with grazing running high up onto the mountain) in 1858 and in the Lawrence Valley, Stoneschrubie (Erewhon) Station in 1861. Sheep were grazed right to the heads of all the surrounding valleys.

The mountaineers were slower in arriving. The principal pioneer of New Zealand mountaineering, George Mannering, resolved to attempt Arrowsmith after seeing the peak from the foothills of Mt Hutt in 1890. In Easter 1893 he optimistically embarked on a four day trip with C H Inglis and M H Lean, driving a horse buggy

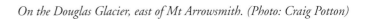

On the Douglas Glacier, east of Mt Arrowsmith. (Photo: Craig Potton)

Jack Pattle on the first ascent of the East Ridge of Mt Arrowsmith, 1953. (Photo: Bob Watson Collection)

Mannering conveyed his enthusiasm to later generations of Canterbury climbers, but in the meantime, the first ascent was claimed by two Aoraki/Mt Cook veterans, sneaking in from the south.

In February 1912, Frank Wright and Hermitage guide, Jim Murphy, headed up the Lawrence Valley – meeting on the way in Tom Fyfe and his friend J Simpson, both from Timaru. They had been in the valley, but had been defeated by the weather and time in attempting the peak. Wright and Murphy were a dynamic duo, Murphy at his peak as a guide and an equal to Peter Graham, while Wright was a superb rock climber regarded by many as the finest professional climber of his time. They camped in a small side valley above the upper Lawrence. Wright wrote: 'we looked forward to an easy conquest'. But in the morning they took a false lead and ended up close to the summit of nearby Mt Couloir. Arrowsmith was over two kilometres away. Wright said:

We had now and then to traverse some very steep arêtes and climb up and down ugly couloirs ... the sound nature of the red rocks stood us in good stead, and Murphy always managed to find some way over or around.

Some 200 metres from the summit they were blocked by a huge tower:

One small chimney leading round and upwards offered. The rope was paid out by foot. Murphy disappeared, coming into view 50 feet above. I followed, breathing freely when the last foot of rope was taken in.

They gained the summit at 12.45 p.m. and thus the 'honour of the first ascent of this somewhat inaccessible peak'.

Other routes on Mt Arrowsmith had to await a new generation. In the early 1930s there was an explosion of mountaineering activity throughout New Zealand. Impecunious youngsters in their late teens and early twenties swarmed out from the cities and towns in search of recreation in mountain areas that had hardly seen a soul in decades. Canterbury climbers looked at the Arrowsmith Range, and Mt Arrowsmith, which along with Mt D'Archiac, was

to Lake Heron, and then dashing up the Cameron, climbing Douglas Glacier to a high col level with the upper part of the South Cameron Glacier. From here they saw the summit 400 metres higher, but a kilometre away across broken ice. They turned for home. But the peak and its neighbours left a strong impression on Mannering:

From the climber's point of view ... may be distinctly called 'first class'. Indeed, do not think I have ever been among such gloriously fantastic rocks. Rugged grandeur dominates everywhere, and the climbing is simply magnificent on the upper ridges.

The Cameron Valley approach to the Arrowsmith Range, with East Horn on left and Mt Arrowsmith behind, Couloir Peak (centre) and Tent Peak at right. Cameron Hut lies in the moraine ridges in the centre. (Photo: Rob Brown)

Cameron Hut – a climber's home, with Couloir Peak and The Twins behind. The access route to Mt Arrowsmith follows the moraine wall (Carriageway) on the left of the glacier. (Photo: Bill King)

the highest peak in the province. Over a period of a year, between 1930 and 1931, there were at least four attempts on the South Ridge of Mt Arrowsmith from the Ashburton Valley. The climbers avoided the more accessible Cameron Valley because the runholder was reluctant at that time to grant access. In April 1930 Andy Anderson climbed to within minutes of the summit alone, but because it was becoming dark and through inexperience he doubted his own abilities, he turned back. Anderson settled the issue the following year however. With Jim and Evan Wilson in January 1931, he retraced his steps. This time the ridge was well iced up and conditions misty. The three made fast time and found only one difficulty, a large tower where they left a fixed rope. The summit was reached at 1 p.m. Their route up the South Ridge became the recognised route up Arrowsmith for six years, apart from an ascent up the hanging valleys and snowslopes above Moses Rock in the Lawrence Valley in 1934 by Doug Brough and Rod Hewitt – an even easier climb than the South Ridge.

The South Ridge fell from favour as the most popular line of ascent once a route was found out of the Cameron Valley. The honour again fell to a Canterbury party in 1937; Stan Conway, Tom Newth, Syd Brookes, Arthur Lees and 'Winnie', Brookes Model T Ford, left Christchurch at 7.45 p.m.. After a leisurely stop for oysters and beers at Methven, they reached the Cameron Valley carpark at 2 a.m.. Setting off immediately, they walked through the night, carrying 25 kilogram packs. By 6.30 p.m. that evening that they had ascended the Cameron Valley, found their way up a lateral moraine (known as the Carriageway) beside the Cameron River and set up camp on the névé below the summit. With an early morning start and a full moon, the team quickly cramponed up a steep snow arête well right of the summit and joined Murphy and Wright's North Ridge. From here it was a matter of scrambling over towers and round gullies to the summit. Keen to vary the climb, they descended directly down a couloir from the summit. Tom Newth recorded,

The snow was frozen hard with an inch of soft stuff on top. The grade was very steep – frequently we moved but one at a time. Our couloir finally petered out leaving us a 100 ft cliff to negotiate before we could gain the glacier.

Their descent route, and a subsidiary snow couloir on its right, are now the most regularly used route to the summit. It is not however, a route to be taken too lightly. The couloir is steep and something of a suntrap. Consequently the snow is often soft and avalanches. There have been two deaths in the couloir, and many stories of inexperienced parties encountering avalanches and falls, battling with soft snow and loose rock at the bottom of the couloir.

Arrowsmith has three ridges. The North Ridge and South Ridge were climbed in 1912 and 1931. The East Ridge, a more difficult proposition, had to wait until 1954. This was a year after the Canterbury Mountaineering Club built a comfortable hut in the lovely surroundings of tussock and grass mats beside the Cameron River near the toe of the Cameron Glacier. The hut was an excellent climbing base, and ascents of Mt Arrowsmith increased accordingly. Nevertheless, the East Ridge was a long climb, and although the hut was used as a staging post, the climbing party set up a tent camp on the Cameron Glacier névé, complete with valve radio to listen to the latest pop songs. The climbers were Jack Pattle and Rob Watson, accompanied by their 'base camp manager' Alan Kelly. Pattle and Watson had attempted the ridge earlier and failed, recording in the Cameron Hut book:

it's bloody tough ... and requires very exact and careful climbing. Good luck to the climbers who pull it off.

In the event, Pattle and Watson pulled it off. They began the ridge early in the morning of 20 February 1954. The ridge comprised three parts, a long flat section of rotten rock, a large outlying knob, and then the final rise to the summit up three rock steps. There was no hold-up until the outlier where they reached a vertical rock face giving access to a catwalk up 'a positively breathtaking narrow section of 100 feet. The view from this and many other passages is truly spectacular'. From here they traversed over the outlying peak and down towards a small col. The rock on the col was positively repulsive. In many places in the Southern Alps there are areas of soft rock, but the rock on the col between Arrowsmith and its outlier must be the rottenest and softest. And from the col rose the first of three rock steps. Pattle described it well: 'The south side of the wall overhung the Ashburton Face, down which rocks were humming like cannon balls!'

The rock on the wall above the col, and on the next two steps above, was however, of reasonably good quality. Once above the first step the summit was a foregone conclusion. The last step, though not difficult, provided immensely enjoyable moves up steep ground and onto the summit. Pattle wrote:

We had reached the zenith of our climb and were experiencing the exaltation that every mountaineer knows ... Not a sound reached us and we relaxed in warm sunlight quietly enjoying the calm and silence.

The East Ridge is one of the most sustained routes on Mt Arrowsmith but not a particularly popular one, especially as the first half at least has poor quality rock.

A much better climb that can link onto the upper half of the

Mt Arrowsmith and the Ashburton Glacier, with the South Ridge (left), Ashburton Face and East Ridge on right skyline. (Photo: Ian Whitehouse)

East Ridge, is the Cameron Buttress, a rock rib which rises out of the South Cameron névé onto the outlying peak on the East Ridge. It was first climbed by Mike Perry and Dave Bouchier one drizzly day in March 1975. Mike Perry's description of the climb records that:

By the time we reached the spur it was raining quite heavily, but the rock was rough and the smooth soles of our friction shoes were not at too much of a disadvantage.

Descending the North Ridge of Mt Arrowsmith. (Photo: Bill King)

Perry and Bouchier had started the climb late in the afternoon, as they feared competition for a first ascent from two others camped below. In the rush they forgot to take water, and, forced to bivouac fairly low down, they spent a thirsty night and harboured evil thoughts for the competition comfortably camped and wa-

tered below the buttress. But their drive had its rewards and next day they completed the climb to the outlier up a series of enjoyable rock slabs. A year later, Rick Burn completed the buttress with companions, and then alone carried on up the East Ridge to Arrowsmith, thus completing the integral ascent.

There remains one other climb on Arrowsmith to describe, and this is probably the mountain's best route. The South Face of Mt Arrowsmith rises above the Ashburton Glacier. By today's standards, it is not a hard climb, but it is nevertheless a good test piece. Unlike other routes on the mountain, it is a snow and ice climb of 700 metres, up a broad snow face and then via a number of gullies onto the summit. The first to venture onto the route were Don Cowie and Jim Clark, in November 1958. It is a climb best done either in late winter or early summer, when there is snow rather than ice on the face, and the 'cannon balls', seen by Pattle and Watson from the East Ridge, are less frequent. Even so, Cowie and Clark encountered what they euphemistically called 'icy meteorites', barrages of which they were forced to climb through. The pair front-pointed their way up the face, using the rather precarious safety technique of belaying from the picks of their ice axes. It is a belay method of bygone days and one which climbers preferred not to test by falling off! Subsequent parties have also commented on the 'odd flying missile' directed their way, particularly on the lower part of the face. Higher up however, where the climb constricts into a series of gullies, climbers can choose either to head out onto the top of the South Ridge, or follow a steeper route directly to the summit.

The South Face is perhaps typical of the whole mountain: easy to get to, nowhere excessively difficult, prone to dangers from rockfall, but on its day and in good condition, a totally enjoyable mountaineering experience.

NORTH RIDGE

Photo: Bill King

MT ARROWSMITH
Classic Route: East Ridge

Access: From the car park near the mouth of the Cameron Valley, walk up the valley on the south bank for four to five hours to Cameron Hut.

From Cameron Hut to South Cameron Glacier (where the climb starts) follow the top of the moraine wall, 'the Carriageway', and up bluffs and scree and step onto the white ice of the glacier just above the icefall.

The Climb: The East Ridge connects East Horn Peak with Mt Arrowsmith. To climb East Horn from the South Cameron Glacier involves an easy snow couloir and a short scramble. Reverse the climb back to the top of the couloir and set out along the East Ridge.

The ridge has three parts: the first is to start off the major outlying peak on the ridge, the second is over the outlier and the third is up three rock steps to the summit. The first third is on poor rock and not memorable. The outlier begins with a rock wall of good rock and then an easy scramble. The final section has a col of dreadfully rotten rock, and then three steep rock steps, the last one just before the summit.

Descend from the summit directly down the main couloir (beware soft snow and a vertical step at the bottom) or climb 200 metres along the North Ridge and descend another, smaller couloir onto a snowslope on the Cameron Face and then down bluffs to the glacier.

Two enjoyable variations on the East Ridge are to climb the Cameron Spur (crux grade 14) to the outlying peak and then up the second half of the East Ridge, or to climb a steep couloir up to the rotten col and then up the last third of the climb.

First Ascent: Jack Pattle, Bob Watson: 20 February 1954.

Grade 3

The South Face and South East Ridge of Mt Tutoko. (Photo: Geoff Wayatt/Hedgehog House)

MT TUTOKO

A lone warrior, Tutoko stands pre-eminent as the highest peak in Fiordland on New Zealand's remote southwest coast, cut off from the ranges to the north by the Hollyford Valley which separates the older rocks of Fiordland from the younger schists of the Southern Alps.

Tutoko stands among the Darran mountains, a range of huge granite walls and deep valleys. Evidence of massive glaciation is well preserved in sharply incised U-shaped valleys overhung by recent glacier cirques and finely-etched summits. The glaciers and snowfields, tiny remnants of their huge ancestors which carved the fiords, are clean and white, unlittered by rock debris.

That the glaciers are so clean is evidence of another natural element that occurs in the Darrans in super-abundance: rain. Successive westerly storms batter the grey walls of peaks with a ferocity greater even than the high rainfall areas further north in the South Island. Rainfall averages seven and a half metres a year. Cool temperatures and precipitation create a low snowline, and in the valleys, dense rainforest grows between sea level and about 600 metres. The forest is montane in character and dominated by beech. The steep, hard, smooth rock walls of the Darrans provide an inhospitable environment which is also exposed to the destructive forces of enormous winter avalanches pouring down from the glaciers.

Above the forests, the snowgrass and the cirques of the Darrans looms the great bulk of Tutoko. Within a distance of one kilometre

the mountain rises 2,500 metres: one of the greatest height gain rates in New Zealand. Tutoko is flanked on the northeast by the Hollyford Valley, rising 750 metres above the Donne Glacier with one edge of the face formed by the South East Ridge and the other by a series of ribs rising from the Ngapunatoru ice plateau. If the northeastern face of the mountain can be described as awesome, then the southwestern side is terrifying. In the extravagant phrases of Samuel Turner, if there were people on Mars, then the most conspicuous sight on earth would be the precipices of Mt Tutoko. The southwest face plunges over 2,000 metres to the head of the Tutoko Valley. The southern edge of the face is less steep and gives way to the 2,500 metres high, two and a half kilometre-long South West Ridge, with its satellite peak, Mt Tauihu. Lying on the far side of the South East Ridge is the South Face, a near vertical series of ice cliffs spawning constant avalanches which feed the Age Glacier. On the South Face's upper edge rises the South East Ridge with three sharp granite buttresses stacked one above the other and linked by sinuous ice arêtes.

With such fierce defences, and situated in such a remote position, it is hardly surprising that the human history of Tutoko is so recent. Tutoko is a Maori name, but was named by a pakeha, James Hector, after a Maori leader, Tutoko, whose family was in 1863 temporarily living at an isolated Maori fishing site at Martins Bay near the mouth of the Hollyford River. Tutoko fed and sheltered

Turner's Bivvy rock, nestled among the precipitous walls of the Tutoko Valley. (Photo: Rob Brown)

Samuel Turner and Frank Milne at Turner's Bivvy in 1921. Apart from a rock wall, little has changed in 80 years (see previous page). (Photo: Frank Milne Collection: Aoraki/Mount Cook National Park)

early European survey parties. To show their gratitude, and probably unknown to Tutoko, they gave his name to the great mountain to the south.

Hard on the heels of the surveyors, a small band of settlers came to Martins Bay. Here they struggled to make a living – and ultimately failed. Those on trips up the Hollyford sometimes reported seeing steam belching from Mt Tutoko.

Later explorers too, described seeing a huge plume from the peak. William Grave noted that:

About four miles [2.4 km] up, where a stream comes in from the north, we obtained our first view of Tutoko, the monarch of this region. We gazed with astonishment. From its summit a long dark streamer rolled away, like smoke from a mighty factory chimney. "Certainly it is a volcano!" we cried.

What the explorers and settlers saw however, was not a volcanic plume, but a great banner of cloud swept by the savage westerly winds which regularly howl around the mountain's summit.

The volcano story did not die easily. In 1895 journalist Malcolm Ross, his brother Kenneth, William Hodgkins and Tom Fyfe arrived at Milford Sound, west of Tutoko, after a three-day hike over the Milford Track. Their intention was to learn more about the mysterious mountain. As a mountaineering group, they were probably the most experienced in New Zealand. Only months before Fyfe had led the first ascent of Aoraki/Mt Cook, while both Ross's had taken part in earlier attempts on Aoraki/Mt Cook and had climbed extensively elsewhere in New Zealand.

Taking their directions from Donald Sutherland, the Milford Sound hostel-keeper, the climbers battled their way up the forested banks of the Cleddau and Tutoko rivers. At the head of the Tutoko River Fyfe became ill and was forced to return to Milford. The other three continued on, scrambled up a creek bed (named Leader creek by Malcolm Ross, ever aware of his journalistic ties as a correspondent for the *Melbourne Leader* and *Melbourne Age*) and then up steep snowgrass-covered bluffs. Their experience with this peculiar form of climbing proved disconcerting, as it has to succeeding generations of Darrans climbers. Philip Houghton, in *Hidden Water* put it this way:

Snowgrass is the curse of Fiordland climbing for there are no safe techniques. The rope is useless, no belays are possible, and boots slip despairingly on the polished grass. One grasps a firm fistful of fronds and heaves.

Late in the day the three climbers pressed on across a broad snow plateau towards a well defined peak at the head of the valley. They must have had a sinking feeling, however, that the enormous peak rising to their left should have been their true objective. Near nightfall, and now assured of an unplanned bivouac before they regained their camp, they reached what turned out to be one of the lower summits of Mt Madeline. Westward rose a fearsome-looking peak of icefall and black buttresses. Ross, employing his journalistic skills to their utmost, described the mountain as the hitherto unknown Mt Fosberry. It was in fact Tutoko. They had climbed the wrong mountain.

So Tutoko remained unclimbed. In 1897 William Grave, accompanied by the Don brothers and A C Gifford, ventured up the Tutoko River. This was to be the first of many explorations by Grave in northern Fiordland. In the next twenty years he mapped large

Looking from Mt Madeline at the South Face (left) and the South East Ridge winding three kilometres from Turners Pass to the summit. (Photo: Gottlieb Braun-Elwert)

unexplored regions, and made many first ascents in the Darrans. In 1897 however, Grave was woefully inexperienced. The party had lost their ice axes before reaching Milford Sound and so fashioned new ones from two oars, some old augers, fossickers' picks, and a gun barrel. With this makeshift equipment, they struggled up the Tutoko Valley:

There Tutoko rose above us – a veritable giant, its bare rock walls towering above us, crowned with a great snowfield, the broken faces of which emitted a deep blue sheen. Ever and anon, an avalanche breaking away, fell with a thundering sound into the valley below.

The peak was clearly beyond the party at this stage in their alpine career, but nevertheless they forged on to the head of the valley and ascended a 1,500 metre couloir running onto the range west of Tutoko. The ascent of the Grave Couloir as it is now known, was no mean feat. But the climbers had been severely tested, suffering an avalanche and a 20 metre fall by Gifford before regaining the safety of the valley.

After Grave's 1897 visit, Tutoko was left to its solitude. Not until 1919 was a serious attempt again mounted. This time the protagonist was Samuel Turner. Turner was a successful businessman whose strong egotism and dogged determination made him difficult to get on with and a figure of fun to many in the climbing fraternity. He was, nevertheless, a sound mountaineer and, given that he employed the top guides of the time, had a climbing record second to none. In 1919 Turner had made the first complete solo ascent of Mt Cook. One of the witnesses of this ascent was Edgar

The spectacular South Face of Tutoko and the Age Glacier, seen from the ridge to Turner's Bivvy. (Photo: Nick Groves/Hedgehog House)

Williams who had fossicked up the Tutoko River in 1917, and now fired Turner's imagination with stories of the unclimbed giant of the south. With typical resolve, Turner set out on the first of five major and often controversial expeditions to tackle Tutoko.

The first Turner Tutoko Expedition lumbered into action. As with all previous attempts, Turner chose to approach the mountain from the Tutoko River. With five others, most of whom Turner employed as porters, the party repeated the Ross's exploration of Leader Creek and climbed the range south of Mt Madeline. In the process Turner liberally sprayed nearby features with his own name: Lake Turner, Turner Falls, and Turner Pass.

Weather and snow conditions foiled Turner in 1919 so he returned in 1920 with Alf Cowling and Jack Cowan. This time he succeeded in climbing the high peak of Madeline. Turner was at great pains to point out that Madeline was previously unclimbed; he had a life-long vendetta with Malcolm Ross resulting from a disagreement between the two following the first traverse of Aoraki/Mt Cook in 1905. In 1895 Ross had claimed the first ascent of Madeline which he called Tutoko, but had only climbed the low peak. Further progress for Turner was, however, thwarted by yet more bad weather.

Turner's big push on Tutoko was planned for 1921. No expense was spared in the much-heralded Third Turner Mt Tutoko Expedition. This time Turner employed Mt Cook guide Frank Milne, a brilliant climber at the height of his powers. The party comprised four others beside Turner and Milne. With two of these, D Macpherson and Norman Murrell, Turner and Milne successfully crossed Turner Pass and set up a tent on the Donne Glacier. From there, the four climbers set out on 20 February to attempt one of the ribs of the North West Ridge. After a late start, they made good time. By 5 p.m. the party were only a few hundred feet from the summit but the weather was deteriorating. At this stage they turned back, in disputed circumstances. Turner wrote in his book, *The Conquest of the New Zealand Alps*, that Macpherson was too slow to let them finish the climb. Macpherson, writing after Turner's death in 1930, said that Turner had refused to let Milne go on, and that a fierce argument had developed between the two. Apparently Milne felt he had been cheated of the peak.

Repulsed now three times, Turner returned home to lick his wounds. And into the gap stepped William Grave, now better sea-

The Darran Mountains in winter. Steep granite clothed in snow, the southern sides of Tutoko (left) and Madeline (right) dominate the skyline. Mt Te Wera and the Te Puoho glacier are in the foreground. (Photo: Craig Potton)

soned in alpine climbing than during his first attempts 25 years previously. He was accompanied by Edgar Williams and Brian Johns. In mock imitation of Turner, they called themselves the Johns Tutoko Expedition. From the Tutoko Valley the three chose a bold new route, up a steep rib on the south edge of the West Face. Grave, Williams and Johns battled up vertical scrub and bluffs and established a camp in an eyrie high above the Tutoko Valley. From there, they ascended onto a large steep glacier and then traversed onto the South Ridge, to be stopped finally by a large rock buttress. It was a valiant attempt that deserved better. The lower section of their route was not to be repeated until 1951, and the buttress on the South Ridge was unclimbed until 1973.

Quickened by news of Grave's attempt, Turner hurried back to his mountain. In February 1924 he secured the services of an-

other top guide, Peter Graham. Turner realised that his best chance of success lay via the Donne Glacier route. To reach the Donne he used an approach from the Hollyford he had proved feasible in 1921. This time the expedition went off with little fuss or bother. From a camp beside the Donne, Graham lead Turner up the North West Ridge pioneered by Milne. At 4.30 p.m., in dense mist, Turner and Graham reached the summit. There was little time to linger, however, and within an hour they found themselves fighting their way off the mountain in heavy rain and wind all the way back to their tent. Although they had reached the summit, Turner was determined that unlike Ross's claims of 1895, his ascent was not going to be disputed. Two days later he and Graham repeated the climb. Graham photographed Turner on his knees on the summit, his ambition to climb Tutoko realised. As historian John Pascoe

Descending the upper section of the South East Ridge – climbing perfection. (Photo: Peter Crampton)

wrote of Turner:

it would please him that his name is inseparably linked with the giant above the sea that extended him to his most dogged tenacity. The glory of his endurance must outlive his vanity.

With the departure of Turner in 1924, Tutoko returned to its isolation. The saga of Turner's attempts and the arduous approach marches gave the mountain a reputation as a tough objective. But in the 1930s, as New Zealand emerged from economic depression and mountain recreation boomed, a growing number of young climbers active in ranges to the north and east became increasingly interested in the solitary, dark bulk above the lower Hollyford Valley. Turner's route via the North West Ridge was repeated three times between 1932 and 1939. Others were beginning to look to more novel approaches.

In 1935 Lindsay and Richard Stewart climbed Barren Peak above the Milford Sound hotel and gained a sweeping view of the western and southern approaches to Tutoko, where the Rosses, Grave and Turner had struggled in vain. Lindsay Stewart was a dynamic and innovative climber with an eye for new possibilities. From Barren Peak he saw potential routes on the West Face, South West Ridge and South East Ridge. The line he favoured most however, was an all snow route from the Age Glacier up the edge of the South Face. Seventeen years were to elapse, however, before he was to rub noses with the route:

In those days we had the existing world of the Central Darrans, all unclimbed and asking to be explored. So naturally the priorities were to get into them first … and then begin to think about the unclimbed routes on the climbed peaks.

Lindsay Stewart was not the only one with ambitions towards Tutoko. During the 1920s a road gradually crept from Lake Te Anau into the Hollyford. Then in 1935, during the Depression, workers began painstakingly chipping a tunnel through the solid granite under the Homer Saddle into the steep headwaters of the Cleddau River. The building of the road and the tunnel was an epic of human toil and perseverance. Tunnellers had to live with torrential rains, thick forest and, in the winter, devastating avalanches which blasted road works, tossed aside heavy machinery and destroyed huts. One avalanche killed two workmen. It wasn't until 1953 that the tunnel was completed and the road finally reached the hotel at Milford Sound. Instead of travelling for three days over the Milford Track, tourists could reach the Sound by road in a matter of hours. For climbers, a whole new mountaineering world in the Darrans was opened up. The western approaches to Tutoko were now within easy reach for many.

The first to take real advantage of the road was Roland Rodda.

In 1948 he climbed the impressive Grave Peak west of Tutoko. In 1949 he and three others attempted Tutoko via the Grave Couloir but were driven back by storms. From the couloir, Rodda saw a rib jutting out of the south side of the West Face of Tutoko. It was the same rib that Grave himself had seen, and attempted in 1922. Thirty years later, in 1951, Rodda, accompanied by Jack Ede, Graham Ellis and Geoff Longbottom followed in Grave's footsteps. Over a two-day period they hacked a rough track up the thick scrub on the lower part of the rib. Then it was a matter of packing supplies up to where the route joined a large snowfield. Here they found evidence of their predecessors:

to our amazement we found ourselves looking at a rusty tin. It was lying in a rough bivouac which we concluded was made by Grave and Williams.

Choosing a camp site 400 metres higher, the foursome settled down for the night. In the morning they climbed up the snowfield, avoiding Grave's mistake of the easier-looking traverse to the South West Ridge, and tackled steep bluffs. A series of gullies led them through these obstacles, onto the top of the ridge and, on a fine late January day, they reached the summit.

Rodda's route was soon repeated by others, but the climb for some reason has never become popular. That claim has fallen to two routes on the south side of the mountain, the South Face and the South East Ridge. In 1952 Lindsay Stewart was at last able to attempt the line on the South Face he had spied out in 1935. With Colin Lea and Jim Ryan, Stewart started up the Age Glacier on a shelf under the South East Ridge. The route was threatened by the possibility of ice-avalanches, but being an all-snow route, they were able to make fast time. Surmounting a steep ice ridge, they emerged onto relatively easy-angled slopes. A wearisome plod in the heat of the midday sun took them finally to the summit. They had discovered probably the easiest way up Tutoko, even if it wasn't the safest. Early in summer, when the mountain is encrusted in snow and ice, the route is climbable and a fast way up. It is little wonder that the first winter ascent of Tutoko, by Bruce Clark, Jim Strang and Paul

Corwin, was via the South Face, or that this was the route of a ski descent by Geoff and Chris Wayatt.

Beside the South Face lies the South East Ridge, one of the most splendid features on the mountain. Viewed end-on it looks fearsome, 'a line of vertical black buttresses'. A profile though reveals three steep but eminently climbable ribs linked by narrow snow arêtes and capped by a winding kilometre-long snow ridge. First to ascend the route were two Americans, Peter Robinson and Dick Irwin, and two Darrans locals, Gerry Hall-Jones and Lloyd Warburton. Robinson had sampled Darrans rock in 1955 and knew that the South East Ridge would provide a great challenge. Hall-Jones wrote:

Peter Robinson did in fact initiate the idea of climbing the S.E. Ridge. Lloyd and I had intended to tackle Tutoko some day but hadn't decided which way. Peter had met Len Kitson at Otago University. Len was Lloyd's nephew, hence the introduction to Lloyd, and Lloyd brought me in to make up the four ... Dick Irwin was much more experienced and had just been to the Andes.

This powerful combination attacked the ridge in 1956. They found to their delight that the buttresses presented perfect climbing enlivened by the exhilaration of vertical drops on both sides into the Age and Donne glaciers. The ridge was a climber's dream; steep, sound rock and exposed positions, all on the highest peak in the district. It was a landmark ascent on Tutoko and became an established classic among New Zealand climbing routes.

Two more ridge routes followed after the ascent of the South East Ridge. In 1959 Mike Gill and Phil Houghton descended the North Ridge, a route of mixed quality which the pair mistook for the frequently ascended North West Ridge climbed by Turner. In 1973 Dick Price and Conway Powell, part of the third generation of young Dunedin climbers, tackled the massive South West Ridge. This feature sweeps 2,500 metres to the summit from the junction of Leader Creek and the Tutoko River. Lower down the ridge forms a subsidiary peak, named Tauihu or the Prow, and is covered first by forest and higher by snow tussock. Above the vegetation a long

On the first ascent of the direct route on the Donne Face of Tutoko.
(Photo: Richard Thomson/Growing Wild)

and success.

With mountaineers constantly seeking new challenges, it seems surprising that some of the big face routes on Tutoko have been so neglected. Lindsay Stewart's climb skirts only the edge of the main South Face. A variation has been climbed onto the South East Ridge up the edge of the Donne Face. In 1968 Murray Jones and Harold Jacobs climbed out of the head of the Tutoko River to the Ngapunatoru Plateau to climb the North West Ridge. A short dramatic buttress high on the right side of the Donne Face was climbed by Dave Vass, Richard Thomson and Rick Turner in February 2002. Although only about eight rope lengths long, the route followed a clean steep line direct to the summit, with superb hard rock climbing in a spectacular location.

A cavalier attempt has been made on the enormous West Face. Pete Moore, Butch Hill and Dave Bourchier put in a four day epic in 1974. They started from near the head of the Tutoko Valley and climbed on a diagonal traverse into the centre of the face. After three bivouacs and continuous climbing, they felt they were within striking distance of the summit. Fate intervened, however, in the form of a rain storm, and rocks loosened from the upper slopes battered the climbers. They began rappelling down. Seventy-two rappels later they reached the valley.

And so Tutoko retains many challenges. There is a direct line on the South Face, but one that may carry a severe avalanche danger. More, longer routes remain to be climbed on the Donne Face. The greatest challenge of the future, however, probably lies on the West Face, especially in winter. Whatever new ways on to the mountain will be tried, Tutoko will always remain a redoubtable old warrior. The sudden weather changes from the west can spell disaster for what otherwise might promise to be a successful ascent. The routes to the summit are all long, and the climber must spend time away from the safety of a camp or bivouac. Tutoko will never look benignly on those who approach him lightly.

snow couloir leads to the foot of a prominent rock buttress. This is the same obstacle which had defeated Grave, Williams and Johns when they climbed from the West Face in 1922. Price and Powell found the buttress split by a deep ice-filled chimney. After a hard struggle they scaled the chimney and emerged onto the upper ridge

Labels on image: SOUTH FACE, THIRD STEP, SECOND STEP, FIRST STEP, TO TUNERS PASS, AGE GLACIER

Photo: Bill King

MT TUTOKO
Classic Route: South East Ridge

Access: From the Milford Highway road it is a long, hard day's walk up the Tutoko Valley and up steep bluffs on the true left of Leader Creek to Turner's bivvy rock. The bivvy is nestled in a tiny cirque west of the crest of the ridge ascended from Leader Creek.

The Climb: Climb from the bivvy, traverse across the glacier (beware of ice fall) to the large basin under Mt Madeline and then gain under the South East Ridge either from Turner Pass or via an exposed steep snow traverse (often badly broken later in summer) to the col at the foot of the ridge. The traverse from Turner Pass is long, time consuming and involves a final abseil to the col at the foot of the ridge.

Ascend the three rock buttresses (superb climbing and the crux of the route). The third buttress is the most difficult at grade 14. Then a winding, undulating snow ridge leads to the summit.

It is probably best to descend the same way, rappelling the buttresses. The route is a very long day's climbing. Beware sudden weather changes.

First Ascent: Peter Robinson, Dick Irwin, Lloyd Warburton, Gerry Hall-Jones: 8 January 1956

Grade 3+

Behind the Marks Flat bivvy rock rise bluffs, the Hooker Glacier and Mt Hooker itself, with a westerly cloud banner streaming from the summit. (Photo: Shaun Barnett/Black Robin Photography)

MT HOOKER

Joseph Dalton Hooker was one of the pre-eminent botanists of the nineteenth century. Yet, given that he never saw Mt Hooker, how did his name become linked with a beautiful mountain in the remote wilderness of South Westland?

Hooker was a scientist who participated in one of the greatest naval explorations of the time, under the command of James Clark Ross. In 1842, aboard the HMS *Erebus* and HMS *Terror*, Hooker visited the Bay of Islands and the subantarctic Auckland Islands before commencing an epic journey to the Antarctic. Without doubt Hooker's descriptions of New Zealand plants and his later associations with Charles Darwin helped lay the foundation of modern science in this country. Of course, none of this explains how Mt Hooker got its name. The answer, once again, lies with Julius von Haast, the scientist whose explorations of New Zealand contributed greatly to European understanding of New Zealand's natural world. Haast promoted his scientific accomplishments by applying liberally the names of famous European scientists from his day, most of who had never visited these shores, to features of the landscape. At least in naming Mt Hooker, Haast chose someone with a direct connection with New Zealand.

Mt Hooker is a beautiful rock and ice pyramid at the southern end of the Hooker Range, a range of singular peaks that runs parallel to and west of the Main Divide. To the east the Landsborough River flows north–south; to the west, the Otoko and Paringa rivers flow directly to the Tasman Sea. Because of its height and proximity to the Tasman, Mt Hooker is very exposed to the prevailing weather systems that pour across the sea. Girdled on its southern aspects by the broad expanses of the Hooker Glacier, Mt Hooker draws admiration from all who see it. Most of those who view the mountain do so from the Haast highway at the junction of the Landsborough and Haast rivers, the very place where Haast first sighted and sketched the peak.

It was from here that goldminers like G M Hassing and William Docherty began scratching around its base (without discovering gold) and the surveyors Gerhard Mueller and Charlie Douglas mapped the surrounding area. Each of these parties visited Marks Flat, a sublime tussock grassland haven below the south side of the mountain at an altitude of 700 metres. Bounded by the Solution Range to the east, and Mt Hooker's glowering cliffs and hanging glaciers to the north, arriving at Marks Flat is always a delight if not a relief after several hard days struggle through the area's remote and rugged landscape. And at the western end of the flat, near where it drains into a gorge of the Clarke River, there are at least three huge boulders that provide secure shelter.

Few details are known about the first ascent of Mt Hooker because the leader of this ascent died before he recorded the details. In late 1928 the ubiquitous Samuel Turner came up the Landsborough with his son Cyril. We can assume that he received

The sun sets behind the beautiful pyramid of Mt Hooker. (Photo: Craig Potton)

Top: Stan Conway, John Pascoe and Ray Chapman on the summit, 1955.
(Photo: J D Pascoe Collection, Alexander Turnbull Library)
Above: Ascending the long, easy slopes of the Hooker Glacier, with the lower
Landsborough Valley in the background. (Photo: Geoff Spearpoint)

ant of the Turner family comes forward with old notes or letters. Until then, we have to assume that the Turners did in fact climb the mountain, which is highly likely. Turner had a great climbing record, even if he did over-inflate his prowess in his book *The Conquest of the New Zealand Alps*. He had climbed the hardest routes of the day with premier guides like Peter Graham and Frank Milne. He had made the first ascent of Mt Tutoko, a much more difficult mountain than Hooker. It is also assumed the Turners climbed Hooker from the south, up the Landsborough and Clarke, and probably then sidled high above Marks Flat and up the Hooker Glacier. The short final western ridge leads not to the high peak, but a subsidiary summit, followed by a tricky vertical rotten rock descent. There is a short sneaky alternative though. At the foot of the ridge a rock terrace leads north on to a high flat hanging glacier. A short distance across the glacier is a rock face of loose, but fairly easy rock climbing some 200 metres to the summit. Maybe this was Turner's route. It certainly was the way used by subsequent parties.

Why did Turner not write up his climb? After all, he had always widely publicised his activities in the past. The answer is that he never had the opportunity. Turner, who had just turned 60 died suddenly of a heart attack on his return home to Wellington.

The second ascent of Mt Hooker, in March 1937, followed the assumed Turner route and involved an early use in New Zealand of aircraft for climbing access. Marie Scott and Dora De Beer, with guides Chris Pope and Joe Fleurty, were flown to the Landsborough junction, accompanied by Alan Cron who helped carry loads before returning to fly back to the Haast township. The foursome approached the mountain via the Clarke River, Murdock Creek, and a sidle above Marks Flat to the Hooker Glacier and then on to the summit via the rock terrace and hanging glacier. On their return to their bivouac they toasted Sir Joseph Dalton Hooker and 'Dora and I [Marie Scott] decided we were two fortunate women'.

The route from the Hooker Glacier to the summit used by

support from packhorses, and local Haast people, and that he had got information about the lie of the land from deer hunters who had been active in the lower Landsborough since the early 1920s. And what was his route? We won't know until perhaps a descend-

this group is now the standard finish to the three most common approaches to Mt Hooker. The most direct route lies up Otoko Valley and Jack Creek. This involves steep work through thick forest and alpine vegetation until the west of Mt Hooker range, between Lantern Peak and Mt Jack, is reached. Then the ascent simply links snowfields and glaciers onto the upper Hooker Glacier. It still involves two to three days hard tramping and climbing. The most popular way in, however, is from the east: either via the Haast highway and up the Landsborough, or from Canterbury via the Huxley valley, over Broderick Pass and down to the Landsborough. Even from here though, there is still large obstacles to overcome. The first is the notoriously flood prone Landsborough River itself. Then there is a hard slog over the Solution Range. The reward though is Marks Flat. In Marie Scott's words when looking down on it 'Kea Cliffs guard an inaccessible Lost World of a plateau well watered by tarns; Marks Flat is a remote secret little plain...'

Most climbers either camp under the large rock on the southwest side of the flat and start the climb from here, or head up a spur at the south end of the flat for three hours to a high, scenic camping site situated amongst rock cliffs on a gravel and scree ridge just below the edge of the Hooker Glacier. From either site, the climb to the summit is a longish, but not technically demanding day through crevasses and then the final rock scramble.

Mt Hooker does have two alternative, and harder routes up it. The North East Ridge is approached from the Upper Otoko Pass. It was first attempted as far back as 1948.

In January 1962 George Carr, Bruce Jenkinson, Dave Skinner, Tony Nelson and Paul Bieleski set out on the 'long row of pinnacles' on the ridge. This was not easy, the rock friable, and at one stage Bieleski fell while leading. Beyond the pinnacles it was straightforward until the final ridge up to the summit. This was steep and 'sharp'. It was 'an exciting finish to a magnificent climb. The exposure was severe, particularly on the Clarke side with that enormous smooth face that drops down towards Marks Flat'.

The other alternative lies up the western side of the 'enor-

Mt Hooker reflected in the waters of one of the many tarns on Marks Flat.
(Photo: Shaun Barnett/Hedgehog House)

Moonrise over the great shelf of the Hooker Glacier, with Mt Hooker behind. The standard ascent route follows to the apex of the glacier before curling out of sight around the back of the mountain. (Photo: Craig Potton)

mous smooth face'. A route from the Hooker Glacier was climbed in February 1966 by David Innes, Bruce Robertson, Peter Foster and Laurie Kennedy. The rock strata didn't favour them. The description of the climb referred to shattered rock, delicate work to avoid dislodging 'rubbish', and schist the consistency of weetbix.

Undoubtedly new routes on Mt Hooker will be climbed in the future. There are certainly tremendous opportunities. But for many people Mt Hooker is not about climbing new routes. Rather

it is a symbol of wilderness. The valleys around the peak – the upper Otoko, the upper Landsborough, Marks Flat, are all a formal Wilderness Area, free of huts, tracks, and air access. It seems fitting that Turner's ascent went unrecorded. The essence of wilderness is just this, meeting nature on its own terms, with every visitor able to experience the uncertainty, the challenge and the reward of wilderness. The climbers of the future have the opportunity to meet the mountain the way Turner did.

HIGH PEAK   LOW PEAK

OTOKO VALLEY FACES

Photo: Craig Potton

MT HOOKER
Classic Route: Hooker Glacier Approach

Access: Mt Hooker is in a gazetted Wilderness Area with no tracks or huts and no aerial access. The best starting point for the climb is Marks Flat. Getting to Marks Flat involves either walking up the Landsborough from the Haast highway to the Clarke Junction and up the Clarke River, or going further up the Landsboroguh to Toetoe Flat and climbing over the Solution Range. An alternative way to Toetoe Flat is from the Hopkins and Huxley valleys and over Broderick Pass, dropping down to the Landsborough. All three approaches can take anywhere from two to three days walking and involve major river crossings. An alternative is to fly by fixed wing aircraft or helicopter to Toetoe Flat. Even from here, the crossing of the Solution Range takes a day.

Once at Marks Flat, there is a good large natural bivouac rock situated on the true right of the lower end of the flat.

The Climb: From the bivouac rock ascend 200 metres west and cross the large stream flowing down from the Hooker Glacier. Then climb the spur to the main ridge overlooking Murdock Creek. Just where the ridge abuts the Hooker Glacier there is a rock band and excellent campsite on gravel. Above here, get onto the Glacier and ascend easy, but crevassed slopes to the ridge west of the two summits. (See photograph on page 112 for the approach up the Hooker Glacier.) Cross a rubble ledge on to the hanging glacier on the north side of the summits and then up a short 200 metre face to the eastern (main) summit.

First Ascent: Samuel Turner, Cyril Turner, January 1929.

Grade 2 (but the length of the approach would add to the grade)

MT WHITCOMBE

Mt Whitcombe is a peak very few people outside the mountaineering community have heard of. It is one of three mountains, the others being Malcolm Peak and Mt Evans, which dominate the Main Divide of the Southern Alps at the heads of the Rakaia, Wanganui and Whitcombe catchments. Of the three, Mt Evans is the highest and most remote, Malcolm Peak is the most striking and Mt Whitcombe is the most challenging. For Mt Whitcombe is certainly not a beautiful mountain, rather it is awe-inspiring. It is like some enormous primeval slab of stone, tilted to the west to form a face running flush into the streams and forest valleys of the Wanganui River. Over the slab lie a series of broad flat glaciers. The top edge of the slab is punctuated by at least five separate summits, all part of the Whitcombe massif. To the east and north are the most spectacular aspects of the mountain. A steep north ridge forms part of the Main Divide, and, to the east, a huge three kilometre long face, rises 1,500 metres out of the Ramsay Glacier.

The bulk of Mt Whitcombe has impressed all who have seen it. Julius von Haast described it in 1866 as 'a stupendous rugged mass, with turrets, pinnacles and minarets rising all along its serrated edges, and a rocky face so steep that no snow could lie on it'. Later in the 1930s, John Pascoe wrote, 'To the west Mt Whitcombe rose sheer from the Ramsay Glacier, and so held our attention that we were unwilling to dwell on the view of the lesser mountains of the Lyell Valley'.

It is somewhat ironic therefore that such a powerful mountain is named after a man who to all intents and purposes was rather a failure. John Henry Whitcombe was a young surveyor employed by the Canterbury Provincial Council. In late April 1862, as the first winter snows were beginning to settle along the high peaks, Whitcombe and a Swiss guide, Jacob Lauper, were dispatched by the Provincial Surveyor to investigate a pass at the headwaters of the Rakaia. The pass had been described (and crossed to the West Coast bushline) by Samuel Butler and John Baker in 1860. It had also been used by Canterbury and West Coast Maori, but in all probability was not a popular crossing route for them because of the wild gorges on the western side. Maori knowledge of the pass was hazy in the 1860s, whereas details of Browning and Harper's passes to the north were well known. These latter routes were quicker, easier and had better sources of food.

Whitcombe and Lauper soon discovered why Maori travellers didn't favour the pass. The eastern approach was extremely easy, but once down into the West Coast forest, the Whitcombe River plunged to a series of rugged gorges, slowing their travel to a snail's pace. Adding to their problems, the pair were woefully underequipped for the conditions, and had dumped food on the pass in the hope of reaching the coast in two days. In the event, they took 14 days traversing through country which receives in excess of 10 metres of rain a year. Starving, the pair staggered out onto the beach

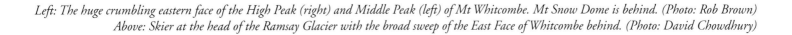

Left: The huge crumbling eastern face of the High Peak (right) and Middle Peak (left) of Mt Whitcombe. Mt Snow Dome is behind. (Photo: Rob Brown)
Above: Skier at the head of the Ramsay Glacier with the broad sweep of the East Face of Whitcombe behind. (Photo: David Chowdhury)

Bob Watson and Trevor James probe for a safe crossing in crevasses, Essex Glacier,
Mt Whitcombe, 1951. (Photo: Bob Watson Collection)

near present-day Hokitika. Throughout the latter part of the trip, Whitcombe had been reliant on Lauper's energy and experience, and each mistake they made appeared to have resulted from Whitcombe's poor judgement. Finally, when crossing the Taramakau River in a lashed pair of abandoned and rotten Maori canoes (a crossing made against Lauper's advice) the pair were swept into the surf and Whitcombe drowned.

This was the tragic background surrounding the pass which von Haast named after the unfortunate Whitcombe. Journeying another three kilometres up the Rakaia Valley, von Haast gazed up the grey moraine hummocks of the Ramsay Glacier at the huge rock face which completely shut off the head of the valley. This was his 'stupendous rugged mass': Mt Whitcombe.

The head of the Rakaia has been a neglected area for New Zealand mountaineers. Its history has been marked by sporadic surges of activity, but the steady development that has occurred in the popular areas of the alps further south is absent. George Roberts and bushman Dan Strachan, crossed Strachan Pass, climbed and surveyed a number of surrounding peaks, and then repeated Whitcombe's journey in just over two days, a truly remarkable feat through untracked country that even today's trampers would be pressed to equal despite the presence of a track and several huts.

But following Roberts' efforts, it was another fifty years before there was another burst of activity.

During the 1930s a small band of young trampers and mountaineers set about rediscovering the mountains of Canterbury. Their great publicist John Pascoe faithfully recorded their triumphs and defeats in *Unclimbed New Zealand, Land Uplifted High, Great Days in New Zealand Mountaineering* and other works. Foremost amongst these sagas was the first ascent of Mt Whitcombe.

On 27 December 1931, under a gloomy rain-filled sky, Roger (Boney) Chester, Bill Mirams, Alan Willis, John Pascoe, Basil Honour and Wyn Barrett set up a tent camp in the Rakaia Valley under Jim's Knob beside the terminal snout of the Ramsay Glacier. That day they had met a party from Wellington who the day before had been to the head of the Ramsay Glacier with their sights set on Mt Whitcombe. The North Ridge of the mountain presented a fearsome snowladen appearance, so they turned back. They doubted whether the young Canterbury group could succeed where they had failed.

As it was, only Chester, Mirams and Willis set off to check out the mountain on 28 December leaving camp at 8 a.m. intending to have just a look at the North Ridge. They ploughed a route up soft snow to the head of the Ramsay Glacier by lunchtime, and after a short stop, headed south along the Main Divide towards Whitcombe, in the process making a first ascent of Erewhon Peak. At this stage they were looking straight at the North Ridge. It 'looked rather ghastly, as most rock ridges do when looked at face on...' Nevertheless, the three pushed on. Willis recorded:

Chester was leading, and struck a sticky piece without a handhold, so we undid the rope, and after several attempts, because of the strong nor'west wind, he managed to lassoo a pinnacle some distance above him. With the aid of the doubled rope while I belayed him, he soon dragged himself onto a safer spot...

A small section from their description of their climb hints that they were perhaps a little out of their depth on this route, but courage showed through. An added complication was a nor'west

The northwest side of Mt Erewhon (left), North Ridge and Mt Whitcombe (centre) and just beside it at the same height, Mt Snow Dome. (Photo: John Nankervis)

storm that was moving in, with cloud obscuring part of the ridge ahead. Nevertheless, by 6.30 p.m. they 'crawled onto the high peak of Whitcombe'. There:

The view was magnificent – we seemed on top of the world. For miles and miles to the west lay a billowing carpet of mist, broken only by the summits of ice capped peaks looking for all the world like coral islands.

Hurriedly building a cairn, they capped it with a brandy bottle (empty!) containing their names, and then quickly hustled off the summit. The difficulties of their climb had impressed them so much that they decided to chance their arm in finding a route south to the Strachan Pass. Their descent proved chaotic, and if the weather had not smiled on them, might have been fatal. They wandered around the Essex Glacier, and on nightfall, attempted to find a route down slopes of scree and avalanche debris into Vane Stream, and hence back to Strachan Pass, only to be stopped by cliffs. It was now close to midnight, but the cold drove them on. They reascended the Essex Glacier and wandered south. 'We ended with the conclusion that we were properly lost.' Fortunately the dawn brought salvation. They discovered a narrow cleft in the ridge and there, nearly 1,000 metres below was the Ramsay Glacier. A steep but not impossible snowslope led down. 'We decided to descend the cliffs. Several times we regretted it, but always managed to keep going.' Thus, by late morning they reached the valley, much to the relief of their companions who, with the threatened nor'west storm finally breaking, had feared the worst.

The first ascent of Whitcombe had been a great climb, made possible largely because of Chester's energy and drive. In reality the party had been too inexperienced for the route they chose, and they had taken some dangerous chances.

The rigours of the first ascent won Whitcombe the reputation as a difficult peak, the 'he-man mountain of the Rakaia' as Pascoe rather exaggeratingly described it. The next three ascents in the 1930s were made via the North Ridge and although the parties rather down-played the difficulties, it is significant that their ascent times were none too fast and only one group made the climb without being forced to bivouac on the mountain. A variation ascent was made in 1946, when Stan Conway, John Clegg and John Pascoe climbed the mountain 'in reverse', via the Menace Gap. This climb was notable for their use of an old bull tether from Manuka Point Station, used in place of their climbing rope which had been lost in the Rakaia River.

Three years later Les Cleveland and Len Brown found a way of avoiding the North Ridge when they 'galloped across the avalanche-swept basin above the hanging glaciers on the North Face of Whitcombe and reached the north buttress of Snow Dome'. Snow Dome is a prominent outlying peak just west of the Whitcombe massif, and it made for an easy climb to Whitcombe itself. Cleveland and Brown's climb was notable for an epic descent in a storm, only by luck finding Menace Gap as night was falling. Barely three months later five Wellington climbers followed the Snow Dome route and then, splitting up, Alex Witten Hannah and Maurice Bishop made the first ascent of Whitcombe's Middle Peak, while Graeme McCallum, Tom Barcham and Ashley Cunningham climbed the highest of the multitude of low peaks, clustered in line about one kilometre from the main summit.

Despite the activity in the early 1950s, it is significant that there had really been no major innovative new routes on the peak. This had to await a new generation. And when the innovation did come, it was truly bold.

The huge east face of Whitcombe which had so impressed the early explorers was regarded as unclimbable by the mountaineers who followed. John Pascoe had described it as 'likely to remain inviolate'. He included a photograph of this face in his Rakaia guidebook however, and to young climbers seeking new challenges, the knowledge that the face was unclimbed was always a temptation.

In February 1962 Mike Gill, Phil Houghton, Ian Cave and John Nicholls established a camp under bivouac rocks beside the Ramsay Glacier, with their eye set on a buttress line that ran straight up the face to the Low Peak of Whitcombe, a 1,500 metre route starting up easy scree ledges and then becoming steeper and more continuous. They were, naturally enough, somewhat apprehensive about the difficulty of the climb, and the soundness of the rock. Gill was the optimist of the party. In *Mountain Midsummer* he referred to a reconnaissance trip in 1960 when, in response to expressions of doubt, he said:

'It's too steep to be really rotten', I replied, developing a theory of mine that the steeper the angle, the sounder the rock. Judging by this the Ramsay Face should be like diamond, but in the event the theory was proved conclusively wrong.

Gill was probably one of the best climbers in New Zealand at the time, having excelled himself on rock climbs in the Darran Mountains, new routes in the Mount Cook district, and the first ascent of Ama Dablam in the Himalayas.

The lower part of the climb was surmounted easily but as they gained height, they were forced to begin placing protection more and more frequently. It began to dawn on the foursome that they had embarked on an extremely nerve-wracking venture. Gill said: 'One's gaze swam about in the dizzy void opening below. On

The Whitcombe massif from the south. The Essex Glacier is on the left, Snow Dome, High, Middle and Low Peaks of Whitcombe, Menace Gap in the centre, and the Ramsay Glacier at far right. (Photo: Craig Potton)

The summit of Whitcombe, from Snow Dome. (Photo: David Chowdhury)

Looking down we could see Ian using his knees. Mike rebuked him, saying even if he was bone-weary there was no excuse for such bad technique when climbing. Ian looked up with a mystified air, 'Climbing? Who's climbing?' he said, 'I'm praying'.

Adding to problems, mist closed in and blocked the view of the way ahead. Then, with the summit still an unknown distance above them, they were confronted by the steepest part of the climb, comprised of foully rotten rock. Gill climbed this section under constant fear of disaster. But on nightfall he finally cracked the climb and reached a short easy snow arête leading to the summit. Gill wrote that later climbers:

will laugh at our difficulties. But they will not see those last pitches, unknown and swathed in mist, as we saw them, nor will they rejoice as we did as they step onto the summit; they will not walk home in a dream; for that sort of experience comes only once in a mountaineering lifetime.

Gill had captured the relief, triumph and joy experienced by his party. And, ironically the route has never been repeated. Their experiences certainly scared off some climbers and the route was made worse in 1970 when huge rockfalls broke away from the left, spewing millions of tonnes of rubble onto the Ramsay Glacier. Perhaps their fears had been justified!

The face has been climbed by a different route since. In March 1972 John Stanton and Bryan Pooley climbed a rib direct to the Middle Peak of Whitcombe. This climb too, proved that in summer conditions, the Ramsay Face could be an evil place. Stanton wrote: *'Steep gullies on either side of the rib roared continuously as rock upon rock fell, bringing back memories of the Eiger to Bryan'.*

Pooley's crash helmet was smashed on the climb, and, later, after their descent, he swore never to go near the mountain again.

And yet, while the Ramsay Face is hideously loose when clear of snow, there is a time, during winter, when snow and ice freezes everything in place and long ice gullies and snowfields cover the rubble and scree. This may well be the time to seek a superb mountain experience but such an event awaits climbers of the future.

either side were flanks of smooth grey wall, while above, the upper part of the face looked dark and menacing'. Gill wrote later, 'seldom have I felt so small and insecure as there, clinging to that vast featureless face'. And yet higher still, Phil Houghton was to describe in the *New Zealand Alpine Journal* a situation that has become a classic in New Zealand mountaineering:

WHITCOMBE HIGH PEAK

SNOWDOME

EREWHON

RED LION PEAK

EVANS GLACIER

Photo: John Nankervis

MT WHITCOMBE
Classic Route: North Ridge – Menace Gap Traverse

A true classic route on Mt Whitcombe is still waiting to be done, probably up the Ramsay Face in winter. In the meantime the traverse offers an interesting, long day's climbing.

Access: The North Ridge of Mt Whitcombe is reached from Erewhon Col at the head of the Ramsay Glacier. To reach the col from the east is a long day's walk up the Rakaia Valley of some 12 hours. There are two alternatives to the col. The longest, but surest route is via the Ramsay Glacier. A shorter route, but subject to crevasse and snow conditions, is up the Lauper Stream, Whitcombe Pass and the Sale Glacier.

The Climb: Approach the North Ridge from Erewhon Col by climbing over Erewhon Peak (although in good snow conditions it is possible to use the Evans Glacier on the west side of Erewhon Peak). At the foot of the North Ridge is a small col, from where the ridge rises to the summit in a continuous sweep. The route is relatively easy and the rock uncharacteristically sound for Mt Whitcombe. From the summit traverse the head of the Essex Glacier (beware of West Coast mist) to reach a short 'sinister' gap between Mt Whitcombe and Mt Roberts. The gap (Menace Gap) has a steep ice slope leading down to easier-angled snow slopes on the south side of the Ramsay Face of Mt Whitcombe. From these snow slopes a route can be found through bluffs to the moraine of the lower Ramsay Glacier.

First Ascent: Roger Chester, Bill Mirams, Alan Willis: 28 December 1931

Grade 2+

MT EVANS

The 1959 New Zealand Alpine Journal contains a very apt description of Mt Evans:

It is an isolated massif and has a beauty and grandeur all of its own; from great black cliffs, steep razor-sharp ridges and curving snow arêtes fringed with sneering blue cornices.

Mt Evans is probably one of the least-climbed major summits in New Zealand. Located just west of the Main Divide it is often hidden in mists while neighbouring summits are clear. The mountain is further guarded by gorged river valleys and dense forest.

The country around Mt Evans is tied up with the activities of two men, George Roberts and Charlie Douglas. Roberts was a member of the Westland Survey for 40 years. He rose to head the Survey and under his leadership the heights of the main peaks were fixed and the entire West Coast mapped. In 1880 Roberts and Dan Strachan mapped the gorges, forests and peaks of the Wanganui and Whitcombe valleys. Roberts then encouraged Douglas, his close friend and employee, to continue the work. Roberts described his relationship with Douglas as one between 'two human beings who fully understood each other and ignoring our many weaknesses fully appreciate the remainder'. Douglas explored up the fearsome gorges of the Waitaha River, and explored further in the Whitcombe Valley, sketching remarkable views of Mt Evans from the upper valley.

It was probably Roberts who named Mt Evans. Its name is believed to have come from a Mr Evans who had done pioneer work in the Waitaha River, climbed to the head of the Wanganui River in the 1870s, and had taken up a cattle run in the Wanganui River. Mr Evans Snr was the builder of the Red Lion Hotel of Hokitika, an oasis that was not forgotten by the surveyors of the area.

Mt Evans shifted from being a triangulation point for surveyors to an objective for mountaineers in the 1930s. The peak became something of an obsession for one of these mountaineers. John Pascoe first attempted the peak from the Bracken Snowfield in 1931, but was turned back. Pascoe was not a brilliant climber but, determined to 'get' the unclimbed peak, he mounted a whole series of attempts with other, stronger mountaineers. Finally, in January 1933, he was successful. Led by Gavin Malcolmson and Priestly Thomson, Pascoe started up from Cave Camp near the Wilkinson River–Whitcombe Valley junction. They climbed snow couloirs on the north flank and gained the upper North Ridge. From here they had to traverse three rock towers. Reaching the summit at 3.15 p.m., they realised they had burned their boats and would have to find an easier way off the mountain. They set off down the South Ridge, and suffered a cold benightment on Red Lion Col. From here they descended to the untrodden County Glacier, back up over MacKenzie Col, and then back to their camp.

Pascoe's interest in Evans lead him to be somewhat defensive about his descriptions of the mountain. Articles he wrote in the

Left: The 1,500 metre face of Mt Evans rising from the Wilkinson Valley, broken by the Lower and Upper Shelf glaciers. (Photo: Craig Potton)
Above: Cloud streamers on the East Ridge of Mt Evans. (Photo: David Chowdhury)

Sunrise on the eastern side of Mt Evans, with East Ridge at left, the unclimbed North East Face, and the North East Ridge on the right. (Photo: Rob Brown/Hedgehog House)

1930s record that 'this is not an over-rated climb'. The issue obviously caused further gossip in mountaineering circles when two Rover scouts, L Wooles and I Cardell romped up and down the unclimbed East Ridge in December 1940, the route attempted by Pascoe in 1931 and named by him 'the Golden Road'. Wooles and Cardell found the climbing 'interesting and straightforward, although rather hazardous owing to the loose rock'. Later climbers would echo the sentiments about the ridge's rock but not necessarily about it being straightforward. Nevertheless, the East Ridge has since become the most climbed route (and includes a variation via a snow shelf on the south flank) because of its closeness to the Bracken Snowfield and the easy but long approach up the Rakaia Valley.

Mt Evans had two more unclimbed great ridges: the North East Ridge and the North Ridge. The North East Ridge was climbed in December 1955 by David Elphick, Mike White, Barry Smith and Jim Wilson. They approached the ridge from the Shelf Glacier, high on the North East Face of the mountain. The ridge has a ferocious profile of five huge rock towers. The team found these were superb climbing, however, and the climbing was on fairly firm rock. On the top of the fifth tower, the atmosphere of the climb

Climbers on the Katzenbach Ridge admire the icefalls of the Shelf Glaciers and Mt Evans, rising above the Wilkinson Valley. (Photo: Geoff Spearpoint)

changed. Jim Wilson wrote:

A cool wind wrapping tentacles of the inevitable mist around us, brought with it fears of a storm and the realisation of the distance still to go.

The climbers raced over the high peak, and fearing a night out, gambled on a risky, quick descent down a soggy snowed-up East Ridge. The gamble paid off and they reached their camp on

Erewhon Col at 10 p.m.

Jim Wilson returned three years later with Tony Evans for the North Ridge. Using Pascoe's old campsite in the Wilkinson they climbed to MacKenzie Col and up steep snow, first on the MacKenzie and then on the County sides of the ridge. They turned a large rock tower via the County side and, from here, were climbing on the route of the first ascent of the mountain. The towers that Malcolmson had struggled up in 1933 were covered in heavy snow. Wilson wrote that:

The final part of the ridge to the north peak rose like a billowing cumulus cloud, for the pillars were heavily iced up.

They followed the first ascent party's descent route via the County and MacKenzie. The North Ridge was a fitting epitaph to Tony Evans who lost his life the following year traversing from Mt Tasman to Mt Cook.

Since the ascent of the North Ridge in 1958 there have been no more new climbs on Mt Evans. Both the Wilkinson (north) and County (south) faces offer possibilities, but the County side at least has repulsively rotten rock. Mt Evans remains an expeditioner's mountain. It is at least a day's walk from any road end. And all too often the mountain will decide it is not available for the day, and Mt Evans will withdraw into its splendid isolation.

A climber carves his way to the summit of Mt Evans through ice flutings above Red Lion Col. (Photo: Eric Saggers)

EAST RIDGE

BRACKEN
SNOWFIELD

LOWER SHELF
GLACIER

Photo: Craig Potton

MT EVANS
Classic Route: North East Ridge

Access: There are two ways to approach the ridge. The first is up the Wilkinson Valley from the Whitcombe Valley. To reach the Wilkinson is at least a day's walk either via the Rakaia Valley and Whitcombe Pass or two days up the Whitcombe Valley from the West Coast. From the Wilkinson climb up the lower sections of the ridge, keeping on the MacKenzie Glacier side of the ridge.

The second way to approach the ridge is from the Bracken Snowfield. The snowfield is reached via the Rakaia Valley, up the Ramsay Glacier and over Erewhon Col, or up the Lauper Stream, Sale Glacier and Erewhon Col. From the Bracken Snowfield, climb a steep narrow gully onto the Shelf Glacier below the North East Face of Mt Evans. Cross the Shelf to gain the North East Ridge.

The Climb: The North East Ridge involves climbing five large rock steps. The rock is reasonably firm and wherever the climbing becomes too severe, an alternative can usually be found on the MacKenzie Glacier side of the towers. Each tower rises

progressively up the ridge, before a final rock section leading to a junction point between the North East and North ridges. The route then traverses the northern peak of Mt Evans down to a col, and then over the high peak.

The easiest way off the mountain is via the South East Ridge, but this will entail a long trek back to the starting point via Red Lion Col and the Evans Glacier to the Bracken, or from Red Lion Col across the County Glacier over MacKenzie Col and down the MacKenzie Glacier. A quicker but more difficult descent route is the East Ridge.

First Ascent: David Elphick, Mike White, Barry Smith, Jim Wilson: 28 December 1955.

Grade 3

The southern side of Mt Taranaki/Egmont, with Syme Hut in the foreground. (Photo: Harley Betts)

MT TARANAKI/EGMONT

Mt Egmont floating ethereal and lonely on the unbroken line of the horizon. A B Scanlon, *Mountain of Maoriland*

In his journal for January 9 1770, Captain Cook noted, '...the southernmost land in sight ... being a very high mountain...' Four days later Cook wrote '... saw the peak towering above the clouds, and covered with snow. I named it Mt Egmont...' The mountain seen by Cook was the North Island's premier peak, a solitary symmetrical volcano rising high above dark green forests.

The peak has two names, Egmont and an older Maori title, Taranaki. Debate over whether one name should dominate has gone on for many years and is likely to continue for many more. The New Zealand Geographic Names Board has declared that both names can be used.

Legend has it that Taranaki once rested near the great volcanoes of the central North Island. The mountain battled with Mt Tongariro for the affections of nearby Mt Pihanga. Taranaki lost, and was sent far to the west. The mountain came to rest near the West Coast and was bound to this area by ropes of the Pouakai range. Here Taranaki broods, with its head and shoulders regularly shrouded by storm clouds. It is little wonder that Taranaki enticed Pihanga, or that Tongariro was jealous, for Taranaki is the most beautiful and striking of all the volcanoes of the North Island.

The geological history of Mt Taranaki is different from the legend, but no less exciting. The mountain is an andesite volcano built up by repeated eruptions over the last 18,000 years. Nearby to the northwest lie the Pouakai and Kaitake ranges, earlier remnants of the volcanic activity which has given rise to Taranaki. Interestingly, Taranaki is only a dormant volcano. Although there are no written records of eruptions, there is evidence of ash showers and buried forests from an eruption as recent as 300 years ago.

The geological history of change and eruptive outbursts has parallels in the human history of the surrounding countryside. Maori settlement dates back some 1,000 years. The dominant groups of the area have been the Taranaki tribe, whose area encompasses the west of the mountain and its summit area, Te Atiawa to the north, and the Ngati Ruanui in the southeast. The mountain was a source of food and minerals (such as the red ochre pigment), a place of refuge in times of war, and a burial site for chiefs. As such, it was tapu. There are no precise records of any Maori ascents, but according to legend Taranaki chief Tahurangi ascended the peak to light a fire for all to see, as an act of sovereignty against other tribal claimants.

Warfare was common and reached a crescendo between 1810 and the mid-1830s. In this period the land was depopulated by incessant musket wars, culminating in the Taranaki Maori being driven south and Te Atiawa being decimated by Waikato raiding parties, particularly at the great Battle of Pukerangiora. Into this seesaw scene came the European settlers who founded New Plymouth in 1841 and clashed increasingly with the Maori over land.

Syme Hut rimed in winter ice. (Photo: Harley Betts)

Stars cartwheeling around the South Celestial Pole over
Mt Taranaki/Egmont. (Photo: Harley Betts)

Dieffenbach Cliffs and up a gully on the northwest side of the mountain beside the Heberley Cliffs. Only Dieffenbach and Heberley climbed the last 500 metres up sun-softened snow to the summit. The weather closed in and it began to snow soon after their arrival. Heberley's rough notes record 'we left a bottle with a charge of shot and gun flint we left no writing for we had no materials having left them at the last camp we could not get any view till we descended about 1000 feet from there the sea looked like a sheet of glass'.

Thus Mt Taranaki became the scene of the first alpine ascent in New Zealand's history.

Since 1839 climbing on Mt Taranaki has developed to the extent that it is probably the most climbed mountain in New Zealand. There is road access to three points: North Taranaki, the Stratford Mountain House, and Dawson Falls, all high on the mountain. Although it is still nearly 1,000 metres to the top of the mountain, this access has meant the summit can be reached quite quickly, especially in summer. The record for a return trip from roadhead to the summit is under two hours. Triple and quadruple ascents in one day are made. There have been mass ascents, including groups of over 500. The first of these 'mass' ascents occurred in 1851. Eighty Taranaki warriors climbed to the summit in a challenge to the Atiawa tribe whom the Taranaki feared would try to sell the mountain to European settlers. The party drove a totara post into the summit and performed a haka of defiance and sovereignty.

With these regular comings and goings, it might be thought that climbing Mt Taranaki is merely a stroll. It is not. More people have died on its upper slopes than on any other New Zealand mountain. It is precisely because Mt Taranaki seems so easy that it has this record. The mountain is prone to rapid weather changes. It usually has a snow cover, which can turn quickly to sheet ice when the temperature drops. Indeed, some of the most iron-hard ice of any mountain can be found on Mt Taranaki during the winter months. And its symmetrical volcanic slopes are deceptively steep, gradually increasing in angle with height and trapping the inexpe-

Between 1860 and 1868 there was open warfare, 1865 being notable for widespread land confiscation.

It seems surprising that anyone found time or energy for the pursuit of knowledge or recreation. In December 1839 however, a young German scientist, Ernst Dieffenbach, left the New Zealand Company's vessel *Tory* near the site of New Plymouth and set out to climb the volcano. He made two attempts. On the second attempt he was accompanied by whalers James Heberley and 'Black Lee' (a Negro cook), a local tohunga Tangatu, Taranaki chief Kake, and a slave. Their route was along the Waiwhakaiho River, past the

Ice turrets of the Sharks Tooth, at the summit of Mt Taranaki/Egmont. (Photo: Nick Groves/Hedgehog House)

rienced climber. Over 50 people have been killed on Mt Taranaki – the most common cause of death is a fall, usually down an ice slope.

Despite the death toll, Mt Taranaki remains an excellent climb, and in the right conditions, a major alpine challenge. Some of New Zealand's greatest climbers have cut their teeth on the mountain. Jim Murphy, pioneer guide in the Aoraki/Mount Cook district, who worked for 20 years running the Dawson Falls hostel, encouraged a new generation of mountaineers in Rod Syme and Dan Bryant. This pair changed the alpine scene in the Cook district in the 1930s with their ascents of the Syme Ridge of Mt Tasman and the East Ridge of Aoraki/Mt Cook.

Later generations produced climbers like Pete Gough, who made his mark with a first ascent of the Caroline Face of Aoraki/ Mt Cook, and Nick Banks, the first to climb all face and ridge routes on Aoraki/Mt Cook. Their training ground had been the glittering ice of Mt Taranaki.

It is difficult to identify routes on Mt Taranaki that stand out. To the detached observer they might appear to have a sameness about them. But to those who know the mountain well, routes like Surrey Road, Curtis Ridge, Crater Valley and North Ridge each have their own attractions. It is on the eastern side of the moun-

tain, though, where the greatest challenges lie. Two routes do stand out: Teds Alley and East Ridge. Both rise above the mountain's skifield to a point where the mountain reaches a steady 45° gradient. Teds Alley narrows for a short section, in winter giving climbers the excitement of steep mountain ice for a few rope lengths. The East Ridge is different. Not quite as steep as Teds Alley, it is more exposed, and more continuous. Climbers on East Ridge in early winter grappling with hard ice know they are on a major alpine undertaking which will permit no mistakes. To do so is to risk a 1,000 metre slide, with little chance of survival.

In summer, the East Ridge is an easy and attractive climb. Moss-carpets lower on the mountain give way to scoria slopes and then warm crusty rock leading up to the crater: a friendly climb enjoyed by scores of climbers.

Looking across from the Pouakai Range to the northern side of Mt Taranaki/Egmont. (Photo: Harley Betts)

MT TARANAKI/EGMONT
Classic Route: East Ridge

Access: There are two approaches to East Ridge. The first is from the Stratford Plateau carpark via the Stratford skifield. Walk up the grass and scree on the skifield to the Policeman (a helmet-like rock feature on the right) and sidle up right to the foot of East Ridge.

The second approach is from the North Taranaki carpark. Climb up left towards and around Warwick's Castle and then up left again towards the ridge.

The Climb: Scramble up the rock and scree, keeping to the crest of the ridge. The rock generally is more stable than the volcanic scoria that makes up the rest of the mountain. The ridge becomes increasingly steep towards the top and finishes on the summit of Sharks Tooth, a prominent feature of the summit cone. In winter be careful of the increasing exposure of ridge towards the top.

Descend north from the Sharks Tooth along the crater rim. In summer conditions locate 'the chimney', a hole in the rim which allows an easy scramble into the crater. In winter it is usually necessary to continue to the 'Surrey Road' entrance about 100 metres distance from Sharks Tooth. The fastest descent routes from the crater are down the north side. The best summer descent route is the poled trail down the Lizard and North Ridge, which begins from a ledge on the eastern crater rim at the top of Crater Valley. In winter, when access to the top of the Lizard is difficult, it is best to descend Crater Valley then cross to the Lizard and North Ridge route at about 2,300 metres.

First Ascent: Unknown.

Grade 1 (in summer); **2** (in winter in hard ice conditions)

Mt Rolleston in winter, with the eastern Bealey Face rising up to the Low Peak and the High Peak behind. (Photo: Robin Smith)

MT ROLLESTON

Mt Rolleston is a giant of a peak: not in height, because at 2,271 metres it is much lower than its counterparts further south, but in its complex sprawl of ridges and faces, and the range of experience it offers the mountaineer. Mt Rolleston lies alongside the main highway from Christchurch to Greymouth. Its three summits rear over 1,000 metres above Arthur's Pass, presenting a spectacular view to the motorist. From the road however, it is only possible to see the Low Peak. Further back lie the Middle Peak and High Peak, and together the three summits link faces above the Waimakariri, Otira, Bealey and Crow Valleys, and four ridges: the Goldney, Philistine, Rome and Jellicoe. Rolleston, and its small neighbour Mt Philistine cradle the two northernmost glaciers in the South Island; the Rolleston Glacier between Rolleston and Philistine, and the larger Crow Glacier.

But despite its size, Mt Rolleston would be less notable but for the important fact that the main road passes within three kilometres of the summit, and Arthur's Pass township nestles nearby in the Bealey Valley. Thus Mt Rolleston has come to mean much to climbers, trampers and skiers. It is a backdrop to popular easy walks up the Bealey and Otira valleys and stands rampant against the skyline when seen from most of the nearby valley passes. From Temple Basin skifield, Rolleston's summits pierce the western sky, while for the climber the mountain holds everything from an easy scramble for the novice, to serious snow and ice gullies challenging the experienced. But the mountain is not one to be taken lightly. It is possible some days to reach its summit clad in a cotton shirt and shorts, but within hours it can be shrouded in sub-freezing storms. The mountain has claimed many lives, and will never treat the disrespectful lightly.

The peak takes its name from William Rolleston, the Superintendent of Canterbury Province in the 1860s and 1870s and a man who gave much to Canterbury and New Zealand in the nineteenth century. Thus, in a way, if a peak is to carry a man's name, it is fitting that it should be of one closely linked with surrounding land. The name was given by Arthur Dudley Dobson, a surveyor and engineer. Dobson, following up information from Maori about little-used passes in the upper Waimakariri, confirmed that the pass below Rolleston (now named Arthur's Pass after him) was suitable for a transalpine road. Dobson had drawn his information from Tarapuhi, a chief of the Poutini Ngai Tahu, who informed him that the route had not been used in his lifetime, as greenstone trading parties preferred the easier and better provisioned Taramakau Valley pass to the north. There is conflicting information as to whether Mt Rolleston had a Maori name, but the strongest claimant is that of Kaimatau, a name given by the West Coast Maori. The summit of Rolleston would have been seen from the pa beside the mouth of the Taramakau River on the West Coast, and the name Kaimatau originates here.

The road and rail links which pass by Mt Rolleston are part of a great saga. The road was completed in 1866, just three years after

Waimakariri Falls Hut on the western side of Mt Rolleston. (Photo: Craig Potton)

Climbing the upper section of Sampsons Couloir above Waimakariri Col. (Photo: Craig Potton)

Dobson's original survey. The haste was caused by gold discoveries on the West Coast, and the eastern town of Christchurch was determined to establish a land route to the fields in order to secure revenue from the gold. The first coach on the inaugural run crossed Arthur's Pass in March 1866, carrying William Sefton Moorhouse, the Provincial Superintendent. For the next 60 years, coaches reigned supreme. However, at the same time as the road was being built, controversy abounded about the need for a Midland Railway to also link the east and west coasts. Indeed, for the next 20 years, Canterbury political fortunes were made and lost over the railway. By the early 1900s the railhead had reached well up the Bealey Valley. From there, engineers confronted the enormous problem of digging a tunnel under the pass to link up with the Otira Valley. It took from 1907 until 1918 to construct the tunnel, through seven kilometres of crumbly and shaly rock. The project was taken over by the Government when the original construction company went bankrupt in 1912.

The road, and later the railway, brought Arthur's Pass within easy access of Christchurch and other centres. Gradually Arthur's Pass became a centre for mountain recreation. Early into the field

were the mountaineers. In November 1891 Arthur P Harper, Marmaduke Dixon and Robert Dixon, members of a newly formed New Zealand Alpine Club, rode by horse and cart from Christchurch, and attempted Mt Rolleston from the Otira Valley. They failed due to soft snow, and climbed a nearer lower peak instead, naming it Mt Philistine after one of their horses. A month later, Harper and Dixon's climbing companion, George Mannering, came into the fray, with A M Ollivier and P Wood. They ascended directly from the pass up the Goldney Ridge (named by Dobson after two brothers who owned the Cora Lynn Station in the Waimakariri Valley and who had given him shelter when he was making his investigations of the pass in 1863). For most of the day they climbed in cloud, and so, although they reached a major summit, they found subsequently they had made an ascent only of the Low Peak. The High Peak was not climbed for another 20 years. In 1912 H Thomson, the engineer in charge of the tunnel project, and I Gilligan, climbed it from the Otira Valley up a long snow slope (known now as the Otira Slide) onto the upper part of the Goldney Ridge. Within weeks the climb was repeated by another tunnel worker, J Murray, who ascended the route alone.

When the Midland Railway was completed and a regular train service linked Christchurch and Greymouth, more and more people began to flock to Arthur's Pass on cheap railway excursions. The area around Mt Rolleston became a national park in 1929. The old rail construction cabins provided cheap and readily available accommodation. Guiding services were offered by Bill Fraser who worked on the railway at Otira, and after 1929, by Oscar Coberger at the Arthur's Pass township. Coberger simultaneously promoted skiing in the area, and within three years Canterbury's first ski-field opened at Temple Basin across the valley from Rolleston.

In the meantime, Rolleston itself was providing excitement for young trampers and climbers. In 1923 Bill Fraser and W Caldwell made the first ascent of the mountain from the Bealey Valley. In January 1929 the first traverse of the mountain to the

Approaching Rome Gap and the upper part of Rome Ridge in winter, en route to the Low Peak.
(Photo: Nick Groves/Hedgehog House)

Waimakariri headwaters was made by George Lockwood, R O and A W Page and Coberger. Three months later, Oscar Coberger and S Saville climbed the ridge south of the Bealey Valley and tackled the steep ridge leading up to the Low Peak. The lower part was easy going, across alpine meadows and up two rocky bumps. The ridge then flattened out into a sharp crest, and the climbers found it easier to stay on the névé of a tiny glacier overlooking the Crow Valley. The glacier led them to a spectacular niche in the ridge, the 'Gap'.

From here the ridge reared up sharply and involved a short section of steep rock climbing. Above was a large tower on the ridge (which five days later collapsed when a major earthquake rocked the area) and finally some steep scrambling on rotten rock. The route subsequently came to be known as Rome Ridge (in fact named in 1928, just before the first ascent, by climber J B Nanson after the christian name of a friend).

In summer conditions Rome Ridge is quite a simple climb. It is in winter however, that it provides the best mountaineering experience. The ridge then sports elegant snow arêtes and leaning cornices over the Bealey and Crow Valleys. The first winter ascent was made by Wyn Barnett and Roland Cant in August 1935. They returned proclaiming it a classic route. It is well within the capa-

The Otira Face of Mt Rolleston, scene of excitement and tragedy. In summer a lovely rock scramble, in winter, an alpine climber's delight. The standard Otira Slide ascent route to the Low Peak is on the left of the Face. (Photo: Colin Monteath/Hedgehog House)

bilities of most mountaineers, even at the very basic level, and is an excellent initiation for those wishing to experience the high mountains in winter.

Since the early ascents, Mt Rolleston has seen routes established on almost every conceivable feature. It is hard, within this short space, to focus on any particular one. The Bealey Valley gives routes like the easy Chockstone Route up the true left of the Bealey Face while on the true right lies the prominent gash of Rome Gap Gully. The Crow Valley contains the short sharp Crow Face below the Low Peak and the easy, but in winter avalanche prone, Crow Glacier approach. From the upper Waimakariri the High Peak can be reached via the remote and long Jellicoe Ridge, the Sampson Couloir direct from Waimakariri Col, and the Philistine-Rolleston Ridge. But of all the approaches to the mountain, the best in mountaineering terms, besides the Rome Ridge, is the Otira Face.

At the head of the Otira Valley the broken face rises up 900 metres to the Middle and High peaks of Mt Rolleston. The face is divided by a broad gully that runs down the length of the face from between the Middle and High Peaks, separating the face into two prominent spurs. The route below the Middle Peak is the steeper and more difficult of the two. It is a place where in winter mountaineers can find an enjoyable alpine climb. It is also a place of tragedy. The Middle Peak spur is not a place to take lightly but its easy access from the road (it is about three hour's walk to its base) and northern sunny aspect tempts the unwary and inexperienced into what can sometimes be a trap.

In June 1966, four young climbers were struck by a ferocious storm which turned the route from a pleasant rock climb into a battle for survival in freezing conditions. It was a struggle they, and John Harrison, a member of a large rescue party, lost. This tragedy, one of New Zealand's worst mountaineering disasters, marked Mt Rolleston as a mountain of danger. But there have been others. The Otira Face, and particularly the Middle Peak route, has claimed at least four more lives since.

The reputation of the Otira Face is softened, however, by the

Climbers approach the High Peak, above the Crow Glacier névé.
(Photo: Nick Groves/Hedgehog House)

beauty and climbing joy to be found on the High Peak route. The climbing here is not difficult, but it is steep and long enough for climbers to know they are on a major alpine climb. The rock is warm red sandstone, and with snowfields lower down, and the occasional rock ridge and arête thrown in, along with the enjoyment of arriving suddenly on the High Peak, it is a route to be savoured. The approach to the High Peak route can either be up some steep vegetated bluffs at the bottom or, a better alternative, via a snow couloir which continues to the Philistine-Rolleston Col. A short distance up the couloir it is possible to walk left across a broad snowfield. Above rises an easy angled rock buttress of red sandstone. A variety of routes ascend the buttress, none of which should overly test the competent mountaineer. Once the buttress peters out, a blocky rock ridge leads to the final spur and the High Peak.

Whichever approach is made to Rolleston, it is a mountain that leaves an impression. To the onlooker it is its bulk and size. To the mountaineer, Rolleston holds memories of joy, triumph and tragedy. For so many New Zealand mountaineers Rolleston is their first major alpine experience, and if they stay with the sport, it is a mountain that continues to thrill, challenge and reward.

Descending the eastern side of Rolleston via the Rome Ridge. (Photo: Terry Salmon/Hedgehog House)

LOW PEAK MIDDLE PEAK HIGH PEAK

OTIRA SLIDE OTIRA FACE

OTIRA VALLEY

Photo: Colin Monteath/Hedgehog House

MT ROLLESTON
Classic Route: Otira Face, High Peak Route

Access: A track from the Otira Valley car park on the West Coast highway leads up the valley. It takes two hours walking to the foot of the Otira Face.

The Climb: Climb up a prominent gully on the right side of the Otira Face. The gully leads up around some steep lower cliffs and then joins a broad, flattish snowfield. Cross left across the snowfields to underneath the large buttress which seems to lead directly to the High Peak (it doesn't in fact, but don't let this put you off). Climb up the buttress, choosing whichever line appeals. Three hundred metres from the summit the buttress joins the ridge between Mt Rolleston and Mt

Philistine. Ascend the ridge and up the final buttress of rock to the High Peak.

Descend to the col between the High Peak and Middle Peak, and traverse round to the Low Peak via the Crow Glacier Névé (unless the col has a shrund, in which case traverse the Middle Peak). The usual descent route to the Otira Valley from the Low Peak is via the easy Otira Slide snow slope.

First Ascent: Hec McDowell, John Estall: 1934

Grade 2+

MT SABRE

By God! You should have a crack at Sabre if you want something tough. There's a peak for you! Gerard Hall-Jones in Michael Gill's *Mountain Midsummer.*

The largest and most beautiful of the tributary valleys of the Hollyford River is Moraine Creek. From the junction with the Hollyford the creek rises steeply through a forested gorge until it encounters a massive boulder field, the remains of a rock avalanche which 2,000 years ago dammed the valley. Behind the rock acres lies Lake Adelaide, probably unequalled elsewhere in New Zealand for the perfection of its alpine setting. The lake is fringed by steep grass-covered slopes and, rising higher, serrated granite peaks and small remnant glaciers. At the head of the valley one feature in particular attracts the eye – a sharp mitre-shaped rock peak. This is Sabre.

Sabre is neither large nor stunningly beautiful. But from no direction is there an easy line of ascent. Its two ridges, east and west, are formidably steep at the bottom. Between them lie impressive vertical rock faces. To the mountaineer, Sabre promises an adventure that cannot be denied.

The approaches to Mt Sabre were explored by E H Wilmot. In January 1883 Wilmot and his survey party made the first ascent of Adelaide Saddle at the head of Moraine Creek, and named Lake Adelaide after Wilmot's mother. In 1889 Wilmot surveyed and named Lake Marian on the south side of Sabre. In 1909 Moraine Creek was visited again by William Grave who was seeking a cross-

ing from the Hollyford Valley to Milford Sound. On the trip Grave, accompanied by Arthur Talbot, Alfred Grenfell, and Charles Gifford, was dogged by bad weather. They ascended Adelaide Saddle but failed to get down through the vertical bluffs and grass walls on the Gulliver side and thereafter lost interest in Moraine Creek. From 1909 until the expansion of Darrans mountaineering in the 1930s, Moraine Creek remained unvisited and the peaks unclimbed.

The first to seriously examine possible ascent routes on Sabre was Lindsay Stewart. In 1934 he saw from the summit of Crosscut Peak a possible route onto Sabre from the Marian Valley up the South Face but he never attempted it. In 1936 he pioneered an intricate new approach into Moraine Creek from the road near the Homer Tunnel via Gertrude Saddle, Barrier Knob, and Adelaide Saddle. From the head of Moraine Creek and surrounding peaks, Stewart examined Sabre closely:

We planned to move over the Barrier summit and Jackson (now called Marian), but was never too keen on this rather long route and had a job to interest anyone in coming along. The north ridge likewise required too much time to get on to it so it left the Lake Adelaide face, which I examined very carefully … always intending to go back.

But Stewart, although he claimed first ascents of many of the other great Darrans peaks, never succeeded on Sabre. Thus, while the easier surrounding mountains were picked off, the more difficult Sabre was left alone, presenting an obvious challenge.

Left: Mt Sabre is the backdrop to snow tussock and meadows around Lake Adelaide. (Photo: Rob Brown)
Above: Climbing the perfect granite corner of the Jones-Chouinard route, Little North Face of Sabre. (Photo: Hugh Logan)

Leading up the steep final pitch of the Jones-Chouinard route,
Little North Face of Sabre. (Photo: Hugh Logan)

In the 1950s New Zealand mountaineering witnessed an expansion similar to that of the 1930s. Climbers from Dunedin and Invercargill came to the Darrans in increasing numbers. It was hardly surprising, therefore, that the unclimbed Sabre should attract at-

tention. Competition to make the first ascent grew, with a number of attempts in 1953 and 1954. Finally, it was a party of Southlanders who succeeded. Gerry Hall-Jones, Bill Gordon, Dal Ryan and Bryce Wood set up camp at the head of Moraine Creek in December 1954. Their quest for Sabre was given added urgency by the knowledge that a fellow Southlander, Ken Hamilton, had persuaded an itinerant Scottish climber, Hamish MacInnes, to attempt the mountain also. The two were known to be in the Hollyford Valley with the intention of coming up Moraine Creek after Sabre. MacInnes was a powerful, unconventional climber who, once he saw the mountain, could not have resisted its challenge.

On Boxing Day Hall-Jones and Gordon ascended steep bluffs which guard the lower approaches to the mountain. Above the bluffs rose a superb sweeping buttress. To the left a snow slope led easily to a small col and a seemingly vertical East Ridge. To the right a hanging glacier led diagonally up under the North West Face to another col where the easier-angled West Ridge began. It was this route they were to attempt first. After only 100 metres up the ridge however, the two climbers were repulsed by a 90 metre wall of vertical granite.

The following day Gordon returned with Ryan and Wood to investigate the East Ridge. On closer inspection the ridge appeared to offer more possibilities than originally thought. At the col, they swapped boots for gym shoes and started up, linking up ledges, gullies and chimneys. The climbing was hard and sustained for the standards of the time. After 120 metres they reached a large tower, a prominent landmark on the ridge. From here they inched their way right along a narrow ledge onto easier blocks. The ridge relented and just after noon they stepped onto the summit. At that very moment their rivals, Hamilton and MacInnes were toiling up the valley. MacInnes was to write regretfully:

We consoled ourselves by making the first ascent of the West Twin, a fine peak, though not in the same elegant class as the virgin [Sabre].

The East Ridge ascent had been a major achievement, marking Sabre as one of, if not the, pre-eminent rock peaks in New

Zealand. It is an indication of the small number of active mountaineers of the time, however, that Sabre was not climbed again until 1959. Indeed, between 1954 and 1970 Sabre received probably as few as 10 ascents.

After Hall-Jones and Gordon's failure on the West Ridge it seemed only natural that this should become the next focus of attention. In February 1959 two medical students, Mike Gill and Phil Houghton, arrived at the col between Sabre and Mt Marian to view the ridge. Gill and Houghton were the first of a new generation of New Zealand climbers. Elsewhere in the country New Zealand rock had a reputation of being rotten, and hence best avoided. Rarely was rock-climbing a sport in itself. Gill and Houghton had sampled the snow and ice climbs elsewhere, and realised that amongst the granite peaks of the Darrans they had discovered a rock-climbing mecca. And in front of them that day in February lay the very centre of that mecca, Mt Sabre.

Launching from the col with Gill in the lead, the pair tackled the West Ridge's two steps head on. They found the climbing of the second step in particular a desperate struggle. Subsequent parties have looked with respect at where Gill went – and have followed an easier corner system out over the South Face. Above the second step, Gill and Houghton felt they had the climb in the bag. They sauntered up easy ground, only to be halted by a seemingly impossible overhanging notch. They were forced to abseil a few metres, leaving a knotted rope behind them, and then scrambled the remaining 30 metres to the summit. Gill's bent ring piton remains above the step, a reminder of this pioneering ascent.

The East Ridge and the West Ridge offer the least difficult approaches onto Sabre's summit. Between them lie the sweeps of the South Face, falling 1,000 metres into the narrow confines of the upper Marian Valley, and the shorter, steeper North East and North West faces which both front onto Moraine Creek and Lake Adelaide. At the junction of the North East and North West faces, a great slab of rock juts out. This is the North Buttress, Sabre's most prominent feature. It rises as a square cut prow, with the lower

Sabre from the north, the North Buttress prominent on the left and the Big North Face to its right. Climbs start from the shelf at half height.
(Photo: Rob Brown)

180 metres comprising grassy ledges and walls. Above, a band of overhangs cuts across the buttress forming a barrier to the upper section of clean grey rock.

Such an obvious feature as the North Buttress beckoned climbers from Lindsay Stewart onwards. It was only in December 1969, however, that a group of yet more Southlanders trekked up Moraine Creek intent on climbing it. Ron Dickie and Ralph Miller were Darrans veterans. They had put hours of research into the climb, poring over photographs until they knew its features intimately. The other two were Harold Jacobs and Murray Jones, roped in to strengthen the team. They had already accounted for three important Darrans climbs: the Moir Buttress, the Marian Buttress of Crosscut, and the South Ridge of Christina. Jacobs was the older, a park ranger with an air of dependability. Jones was the young firebrand, a rebel and a loner. He lived for his climbing in the summer and eked out an existence in the winter working on construction sites.

Starting from the Moraine Creek Hut, the four walked around Lake Adelaide, ascended the bluffs and by midday were at the foot of the buttress. At this stage, Dickie took sick so he and Miller called a halt. Jacobs and Jones pressed on, climbing onto the lower part of the buttress. Belaying ropelength by ropelength, the pair were slowly forced leftwards onto the edge of the buttress, 180 metres up, and directly under the prominent overhangs. Jones succeeded in cracking this problem, the hardest part of the climb, by forcing a passage up the edge of the North East Face. Following Jones, Jacobs came close to strangling himself when, laden down with both his own and Jones' pack, and other impedimentation, he fell off. In fact, the pair realised their techniques on this steep ground were rather inept – a fact not lost on Jones who set about furthering his experience overseas. However, they still had another 280 metres to climb and it was dark. They bivouacked on a tiny ledge. The morning brought fine weather and a long, hard haul to the summit. The climbing was sustained but not severe. Both were plagued also by the heat. Jacobs wrote:

My mouth was so dry I almost choked if I tried to swallow. I thought of Moses tapping the rock and tried just that to alleviate my mental discomfort ... We were not the first party to suffer this way in Fiordland with its 300 odd inches of rain each year.

It was only later in the cool of the valley, that Jones and Jacobs could relax, and look back up at what they had climbed – one of the most elegant routes in the Darran Mountains.

East Ridge, West Ridge, North Buttress; what else had the mountain to offer? In terms of the traditional approach to mountaineering, it had given up most of its potential. But when the obvious ways are proved, new possibilities open up. And so it was on the Sabre. The North East and North West faces were untouched.

Murray Jones, blooded on the North Buttress and quick to learn new skills in the European Alps and at Yosemite in the USA, returned to Sabre and began the trend which was to confirm the mountain's reputation. First he ascended a route on the right of the South Face with Roger Thompson in 1969. Then in 1971 he climbed the North East Face with Graeme Dingle. They made an interesting pair. Jones was the more experienced and approached climbing in a determined and workman-like manner. Dingle was a media man, endlessly enthusiastic and conscious always of good copy. As with so many of his climbs, Dingle had the media along, this time a film crew. Their climb, known as the 'TV Route', was superb, on solid steep rock and in sunny, sheltered locations. Its reputation for enjoyable, hard but safe climbing grew with an increasing number of repeat ascents. By the late 1970s and early 1980s new lines were established on the face, most notably the demanding free-aid Ram Paddock Road, and the intricate linking pitches of Sabre-Rattling, an especially fine route climbed by Murray Judge and Andrew Macfarlane. The North East Face (or little North Face as it became known) has become a giant rock gymnasium.

Around the corner from the North East Face is the North West or the Big North Face, a creature of a different breed. It is just as steep as the North East, but longer. In addition, snow patches under the summit leak water under its cracks, vegetation clings in improbable places, and the sun takes longer to reach the big corners and grooves. Climbers in the 1960s and early 1970s searched it for possibilities, but techniques and skills not present in New Zealand at the time seemed to be required. That is, until three young Dunedin climbers arrived on the scene. Each had avidly read accounts of multi-day wall climbs in Yosemite Valley and in the Dolomites and realised that similar, if perhaps wetter, experiences were to be had in the Darrans. The three were Bill Denz,

A panorama at the head of Moraine Creek, with Lake Adelaide in the foreground, Sabre (centre) and Mt Marian with its fearsome 800 metre face. The many faces and cirque walls on Mt Barrier are on the right. (Photo: Rob Brown)

Murray Judge and Phil Herron. They formed one of New Zealand's most powerful climbing combinations of the 1970s, with a determination to succeed that made up for their lack of skill in big wall climbing. It is a mark of that determination that they tackled first the biggest, ugliest route they could find. This was the 700 metre face on Sabre's companion peak, Mt Marian. Denz wrote later:

I just look for the obvious challenge so I don't mind vegetation. Marian was really dirty, and I guarantee that it will never be popular, but it will always have a reputation!

After Marian, Denz's next obvious challenge was Sabre. To Denz, Murray Judge was a perfect complement:

His climbing was so much above everyone else's at the time. I saw he was ambitious and wouldn't stop at what had been done.

Phil Herron was different again. At 17, he was a bright young star, travelling the knife edge between larceny and fierce high spiritedness. A friend Neil Whiston described him as:

a little guy, flying through the summer sun of the Darrans or getting high on Jefferson Starship and dope in Dunedin.

Flushed with success on Marian in December 1974, the three returned to Marian Creek a month later and went straight for Sabre's Big North Face. They chose an obvious line of weakness up chimneys in the centre of the face. Night caught them still half way up, so they were forced to bivouac. Herron and Judge half-hung in makeshift bosun chairs of nylon from ropes and pitons. The climb finished the next day with a typical bold Judge lead up a 50 metre slab with no intermediate protection and the prospect of a 100 metre fall.

Mt Sabre's forbidding South Face in winter, with Mt Marian (left) and Mt Adelaide (right).
(Photo: Colin Monteath/Hedgehog House)

A year after the first ascent of the North West Face Phil Herron had matured into a powerful lead climber, undeterred by steep slabs or lack of protection. In January 1975 he climbed a second route on the face immediately right of the North Buttress. A month later he returned with Judge and Denz to attempt a fiercer-looking route in the centre of the face. Herron was now called the Kamikaze Kid, after his climbing style. The name stuck to the route he climbed with Denz and Judge.

The initial three pitches to large terraces under the face were slabby and hard to protect. Above the terraces a huge flake lay against the face with a chimney on one side. Above this the threesome

encountered steep face climbing, then a roof, followed by a clean-cut overhanging corner with a 30 metre knife-blade crack. This was followed by two further pitches of mixed and aid climbing, then pleasant jamcracks and slabs. Denz led the final wildly over-hanging chimney which ended quite suddenly on a broad ledge. From there it was a matter only of scrambling over easy large blocks and scurrying down the East Ridge as the rain set in.

The centre of the North West Face, where Denz, Judge and Herron battled their way with rope manoeuvres and pitons, is steep and often overhanging. Further left towards the North Buttress however, the rock is less vertical. Here a series of large corners form a playground for those who revel, not in the ascent itself, but in the method of ascent. These are the free-climbers, a new breed of alpinists born on the small rock-climbing crags of Dunedin, Christchurch and the central North Island. On these crags, rock-climbing competition has pushed standards high so that the game becomes vertical ballet, with style all-important. The aim is to complete a climb without resorting to pulling up on pitons or jammed nuts. But to transfer this style from a 20 metre rock near a city to a 500 metre wall in the remote vastness of rain-soaked Fiordland required vision and commitment. One person with such qualities was Calum Hudson. Hudson had spent hours under the North West Face puzzling out a route which might be climbed without resorting to aid climbing. He was not alone either. To many climbers a free ascent of the face was a plum objective.

In February 1982 Hudson teamed up with Nigel Perry. They started on the slabby rock near the toe of the North Buttress and quickly moved over to easy grassy terraces before traversing right onto steeper ground. 'Wearing our friendly haul bag', Perry wrote, 'I traversed to Hudson's lair'. 'Are you ready', he says, pointing upwards, 'are you ready for war?' 'War' was a series of hard pitches, a scoop, a chimney and a wall. Increasingly the climbers felt the space beneath their feet growing. Perry said:

We were up there, miles in the sky above Lake Adelaide, with the sun sheening the [Milford] Sound.

Darkness caught Hudson and Perry in a gully just short of the summit. In the morning the pair scrambled to the top, their route, Sarkasmos, completed: the first all-free ascent of the Big North Face.

The South Face of Sabre is longer than its companion North East and North West by some 500 metres. It is less steep. But glowering above the confines of the Marian Valley, its sunless visage retains the seriousness of a true alpine setting. In summer, its rocks retain the wetness of the frequent rainstorms. In winter, long tentacles of vertical ice droop down its flanks. Murray Jones recognised its massive presence and saw it as one of the premier rock-

Bill Denz crosses a frozen Lake Marian, en route to make the first winter ascent of the South Face of Mt Sabre (behind), 1984. (Photo: Bill Denz Collection)

climbing challenges of the Darrans. In 1971 he and his brother Alan climbed a shallow buttress directly up the centre of the face. Alan wrote:

Murray voiced the opinion that the climb was the hardest he had ever done in New Zealand. The reason for his conclusion was the sustained high-grade rock, the length of the climb on the face [12 hours], and the exposure.

The ubiquitous Denz knew of Jones's delight and in 1978, with Stu Allan, snatched a gully left of Jones's route. The gully, guarded beneath by a half-moon-shaped overhang, had repulsed three previous attempts until Denz sneaked around the ridge edge on aid. A superb wall pitch led into a magnificent 300 metre corner.

These two routes, Jones's buttress and Denz's corner, were both climbed in February, one of two or three months when the face is free of snow and ice. In winter, the scene is different. One climber confessed:

You can lie down in the bivy and look directly up at the South Face. It's the most evil face I have seen, able to crush your mind before you set foot on it. From my previous trips up [the Marian] valley in winter, I've learnt it's important not to look too long.

The climber was Kim Logan, a man with an obsession with Sabre in winter. In 1983 he attempted the face three times, only to be repulsed by weather or rotten ice. The following year he was approached by Denz, with an offer to join him on the North Face Direct of Mt Jannu, a route of horrendous proportions even by Himalayan standards. Logan's reply was, 'if I can't do Sabre, I can't do Jannu'. So they had to do Sabre.

They realised the undertaking was serious. The Darrans in winter represent climbing at its limits. The low altitude of peaks and closeness to the sea mean that ice climbs can turn into soggy waterfalls in hours. Weather can change in minutes, and the steepness of walls brings instant avalanches of spindrift on the steeper walls, and slab slides of gigantic proportions on lesser slopes. In Logan's words, 'the Darrans ice is tough climbing to the limit. I do not know the fancy words to express to you newcomers – "you blow it just once, and you're dead!"'

On a cold winter June day in 1984, Logan and Denz ploughed a deep trench through soft powder snow up the upper canyon of the Marian Valley towards Sabre. A bivouac and breakfast behind them, the pair tiptoed nervously up the lower slopes to the foot of vertical ice runnels. Logan recalled:

15 metres up I placed a screw, 20 metres and came to a dead end. 90° thin ice on smooth rock ... I look between my feet – Bill's looking up. Our eyes meet for a second, then he looks away – nothing said ... No more negative thoughts going through my head, its 100% commitment. It's now or never. I pull on my right hand and lift my right foot and swing out around and up in one motion. Once on the hanging ice

my left hand tool goes in fast, a reprieve. I work fast trying to make my 12 stone weight two. After seven metres and 80° ice, it lays back to 70°–65°. I place a runner. I scream like hell. 'This is war!'

The climbing continued in the same vein for seven rope lengths and then lay back to 'gentler' 65° slopes. At 5 p.m. they reached the summit, to look out over a solid black wall of cloud coming in from the coast. Forty-five minutes later the storm hit the tired climbers and pinned them on the East Ridge. Many climbers might have been tempted to try and push on in the dark. Denz, with years of experience, knew it was time to dig in. They fashioned a tiny snow hole with their ice axes and huddled together, safe at least from the howling fury outside.

The morning was wild, but less severe than the night before. Rappelling down they reached the Sabre–Adelaide Col and descended to the Marian Valley, kicking off wet snow avalanches in front of them. That night a foot of snow fell, and with it further avalanches. Denz and Logan's retreat down valley was menaced by snowslides. Finally, Logan said:

half a second warning then another avalanche hits us. I feel tremendous pressure as it's trying to drag me down. It feels like minutes before it passes. I look up. Bill's smiling at me and says, 'it's good to see you.'... at 4.00 p.m. we reach the car in pouring rain.

Denz was not so lucky three months later, however. A small snow slide on Mt Makalu in the Himalayas caught him and, triggering a larger slide, carried the seemingly indestructible Denz into a basin. He did not survive.

MT SABRE

TO PHIL'S BIV →

Photo: Rob Brown

MT SABRE
Classic Route: North Buttress

Access: Either:

1. Walk up the Moraine Creek from Hollyford Valley and around the true left of Lake Adelaide (4–6 hours), or

2. From the Homer Tunnel walk to Gertrude Saddle, climb three quarters of the way up Barrier Knob, traversing under the Knob on the west, descending, then via Adelaide Saddle and Giffords Crack into the head of Moraine Creek (4–6 hours). Cross the tussock slopes beneath the walls of Mt Barrier to reach Phil's Bivy, one of a group of large boulders under Mt Marian.

The Climb: Climb up the bluffs near a prominent water course. Gain the North Buttress from the left (looking up) via a short, steep grassy step. You are now on the 'Yak Pastures'. Climb up left for two pitches, then for two more pitches ascend the edge of the Little North Face (crux grade 15). The final six pitches head up the centre of the buttress. Descend the East Ridge. A rappel may be necessary.

First Ascent: Murray Jones, Harold Jacobs: 20 December 1969.

Grade 4- (crux grade 15)